The Recorder Today

The Recorder Today

EVE O'KELLY

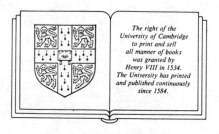

The right of the
University of Cambridge
to print and sell
all manner of books
was granted by
Henry VIII in 1534.
The University has printed
and published continuously
since 1584.

CAMBRIDGE UNIVERSITY PRESS

Cambridge
New York   Port Chester
Melbourne   Sydney

Published by the Press Syndicate of the University of Cambridge
The Pitt Building, Trumpington Street, Cambridge CB2 1RP
40 West 20th Street, New York, NY 10011, USA
10 Stamford Road, Oakleigh, Melbourne 3166, Australia

First published 1990

Printed in Great Britain at
the University Press, Cambridge

British Library cataloguing in publication data

O'Kelly, Eve
The recorder today.
1. Recorder music. Recorders
I. Title
788'.53
ISBN 0 521 36660 7
ISBN 0 521 36681 X pbk

Library of Congress cataloguing in publication data

O'Kelly, Eve E.
The recorder today / Eve E. O'Kelly.
    p.   cm.
Includes index.
Bibliography: p.
ISBN 0 521 36660 7. – ISBN 0 521 36681 X (pbk.)
1. Recorder (Musical instrument) 2. Recorder music –
Interpretation (Phrasing, dynamics, etc.) I. Title.
ML990.R405   1990
788.3'6 – dc 20

ISBN 0 521 36660 7 hard covers
ISBN 0 521 36681 X paperback

WD

Contents

Contents

Illustrations

Musical examples

Musical examples

Musical examples

Preface

The recorder is one of the most widely played, and yet least understood, of instruments. In many people's minds it is associated, not always pleasantly, with their first attempts at making music as children and it comes as a surprise to discover the variety of contexts in which it is now played. The last thirty years, in particular, have seen a very considerable increase in 'serious' recorder playing, as a consequence of the interest generated by the early music movement. The new light which this has cast on the early history of the recorder and its music has served to point up the differences between it and other woodwind instruments and in some measure to illuminate the characteristic qualities that appeal so strongly to its adherents.

Almost from the beginning of the revival in the early part of this century new works have augmented the rediscovered historical repertoire of the sixteenth, seventeenth and eighteenth centuries. The ever-increasing musical and technical complexity of these modern works reflects the rise in playing standards as well as the changing status of the recorder as the revival has gained ground. There is a sizeable repertoire of twentieth-century recorder music in a wide range of contemporary styles, much of it employing innovative instrumental techniques.

The aim of the present work has been to make available to players, composers, teachers and interested non-specialists the sort of practical information they need in order to approach the modern recorder repertoire with understanding. The following central questions have guided the research: In what way does the present-day recorder differ from its historical forebears? By what process has the recorder reached its present position of popularity and who are the main leaders of this revival? Of what does the modern recorder repertoire consist and how does it relate to twentieth-century music as a whole? What are the new playing techniques for recorder, how are they used and how do they compare with similar developments in other instruments?

The compilation of the catalogue which comprises Part II was felt to be a particularly important part of the research, since one of the main stumbling blocks to the further progress of the recorder, and the reason why so many people are ignorant of its full capabilities, is largely lack of information about the music now available for it, music which sometimes takes the recorder into realms far removed from those of the 'flauto dolce' of the Baroque.

The research for this book has been greatly facilitated by the generous help of many friends and colleagues in the recorder world who have given freely of their time and expertise in discussions and correspondence. In particular I should like to thank Frans Brüggen, who consented to be interviewed at some length; Edgar Hunt for his constant support since the very beginning of this project; Carl Dolmetsch for much useful information, and also Ross Winters. I should also like to thank Michael Barker, Kees Boeke, Daniël Brüggen and Walter van Hauwe of the Netherlands; Gerhard Braun, Hermann Moeck and Michael Vetter of the Federal Republic of Germany; Matthias Weilenmann of Switzerland; Cécile Michels of France; David Lasocki, Sigrid Nagle, Pete Rose and Andrew Waldo of the USA and Peter Hannan of Canada. Malcolm Tattersall has made his catalogue of Australian recorder music available to me and Herman Rechberger has allowed me to make use of his research on extended recorder techniques. I am indebted to Frances Palmer, Keeper of Musical Instruments at the Horniman Museum, London and to Robert Bigio for valuable information on recorder design; to Toshio Watanabe for information on Japanese ethnic music and instruments and to Michelene Wandor for helpful comments on the text. Lengthy translations from German, Dutch, Italian and French were undertaken by Ann O'Kelly and Helen Watanabe. Many people on the staffs of libraries, music publishing houses and more than twenty Music Information Centres internationally helped me to track down new recorder music and responded to endless queries. They are too numerous to list individually but I should like to mention Patricia O'Sullivan and Jonathan Askey of Moeck UK, Roy Murray of Schott and Co. Ltd, London and Eric Forder of Universal Edition, London.

Finally, I should like to thank the six people whose practical help and constant moral support has enabled me to survive the vicissitudes that beset the author: my family, namely Helen, Ann, Toshio, Alice, Rose and, most of all, Claire, my invaluable research assistant and mother, to whom this book is dedicated with my love.

Acknowledgements

MUSICAL EXAMPLES

Grateful acknowledgements are due to the following for permission to quote from the works cited.

Schott & Co. for Leigh: *Sonatina*; Hindemith: *Trio*; Du Bois: *Muziek*; Andriessen: *Sweet*; Shinohara: *Fragmente*; Linde: *Music for a Bird, Märchen, Amarilli mia bella*; Casken: *Thymehaze*. Hermann Moeck Verlag for Leenhouts: *Report upon 'When shall the sun shine?'*; Cooke: *Quartett*; Eisma: *Wonderen zijn schaars*; Braun: *Minimal Music II, Nachtstücke, Schattenbilder, Inmitten der Nacht*; Gümbel: Flötenstories, Veller: Nachtarice, Hashagen: Conmon, Heider: Katalog; Du Bois: *Pastorale VII*; Lechner: *Spuren im Sand, Varianti*; Riehm, *Gebräuchliches*. PWM/Moeck for Serocki: *Arrangements*. Donemus for Bank: *Put me on my Bike no. 1, Die Ouwe*; Hekster: *Encounter*; Eisma: *Hot, powdery stones*. Hänssler Verlag for Braun: *Monologe I*; Hashagen: *Gardinenpredigt eines Blockflötenspielers*. Breitkopf & Härtel for Baur: *Mutazioni*. Universal Edition for Berio: *Gesti*. Edition Modern for Furrer-Münch: *Details IV*. Zen-On Music Co. Ltd for Ishii: *Black Intention*; Hirose: *Lamentation, Idyll I*. Hug & Co. for Moser: *Alrune*. Ricordi & Co. Ltd for Bussotti: *RARA*. Jasemusiikki Ky for Rechberger: *Consort Music I*. Hans-Martin Linde for Linde: *Consort Music*.

Grateful thanks are due to the following for permission to reproduce copyright photographs: Carl Dolmetsch (1, 7); London Photographic Library (2); Jean van Lingen (3); Reg Wilson (4); Moeck UK (5); Adrian Brown (6); Britten–Pears Foundation (8); Co Broerse (9); A. von Waadenoyen Kernekamp (10); Maarten Brinkgreve (11); Bas Brüggen (12).

Notational conventions

Pitch: The Helmholtz system of pitch notation is used, with specific pitches indicated by capital and lower-case letters in *italics*. Where notes are given in ordinary roman capitals no particular octave pitch is implied.

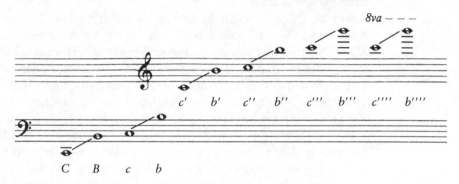

Fingering: This is indicated in the following manner:

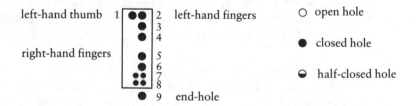

left-hand thumb   1   2 left-hand fingers   ○ open hole

right-hand fingers   5   ● closed hole

                     9 end-hole   ◒ half-closed hole

1 *The revival*

It is easy to make the mistake of thinking that we in the twentieth century have been solely responsible for the revival of early music and even easier to see the revival of the recorder as a sort of fairytale reawakening effected overnight by a touch of Arnold Dolmetsch's magic wand. That the recorder is now so widely played is, in fact, the result of a long and slow process of growth which has not one, but several, simultaneous sources. When one looks at the historical evidence, the roots of this interest in 'old' music, which is now such a booming part of our music industry, can be traced back to the early nineteenth century. Most writers on this topic regard the 1829 performance in Berlin of Bach's St Matthew Passion, conducted by the twenty-year-old Mendelssohn, as a significant landmark in the rediscovery of the music of the past. Nor was this an isolated phenomenon, but rather the inevitable and eventual practical expression of the German interest in Bach and his music which had been growing for the previous thirty years (Haskell 1988, 13–15).

By the 1890s the revival of early music (meaning music of the late Renaissance and Baroque) was well established in Europe. Most capital cities had series of 'historical concerts' which were attended by fashionable society, and large collections of original instruments had been assembled in countries such as Belgium, England, France, Germany, Holland, Italy and in the United States of America. Apart from some isolated exceptions, however, no serious efforts had yet been made to discover how these instruments were made or exactly how they were intended to be played. The recorder was very much in the background, overshadowed by the better-known instruments such as viols, lute and harpsichord.

ARNOLD DOLMETSCH

This well-developed but mainly antiquarian interest in old music and instruments began to give way towards the close of the nineteenth century to a growing feeling that there must be more to these quaint museum pieces that our ancestors thought so highly of. One of the first to see that this music was

1

once a part of the people's daily life and could become so again was Arnold
Dolmetsch (1858–1940) (Plate 1), a French instrument maker,musician and
scholar who settled in England in 1883. Dolmetsch came from a family of
piano makers and organ builders and was thus trained as a craftsman and
piano tuner by the time he reached his teens. The seeds of his interest in old
instruments may have been sown while he was a student at the Brussels
Conservatoire from 1879 to 1883. His first study there was the violin and his
musical tastes as a young man leaned very much towards Brahms and Berlioz.
He did, however, try out some of the instruments from the Conservatoire
collection and recalled attending a lecture-demonstration at which recorders
were played with disastrous misunderstanding of their fingering, resulting in
a round condemnation on the part of the audience of the instruments and of
the unmusicality of the players of those bygone days (Campbell 1975, 12).
This was probably the first time Dolmetsch heard recorders being played, but
it was not until more than twenty-five years later that he began to take a
serious interest in the instrument.

In 1883, hearing of the opening of the Royal College of Music in London,
the twenty-five-year-old Dolmetsch arrived with his first wife and baby
daughter, Helène, to pursue further studies. At the RCM he came into contact
with many great names: J. F. Bridge, Hubert Parry, C. V. Stanford, Jenny
Lind and Sir George Grove, the college's first director. In the late 1880s he
began to be interested in the music of Purcell, Handel and Corelli and his
curiosity quickly led him to seek out the correct original instruments on
which to play the music. He picked up old instruments in auction rooms and,
using the skills acquired as a boy in the family business, restored them to playing condition. He searched the libraries of the British Museum and the Royal
College of Music and unearthed many forgotten masterpieces. In 1891 he
began to give his 'Historical Concerts', in which viols, lutes, harpsichords,
virginals and other early instruments were introduced to the public for the
first time, playing the music which was intended for them in a manner as
authentic as it was then possible to be. Dolmetsch was at this time in his mid-
thirties, a charismatic figure full of energy and conviction. His enthusiasm for
all early instruments and his passionate zeal in communicating his discoveries
brought him a considerable following among the intelligentsia in London,
among them W. B. Yeats, Oscar Wilde, Walter Sickert, Walter Crane,
Augustus John, William Morris, Herbert Horne, Edward Burne-Jones and
George Bernard Shaw. The latter was a consistent supporter and a regular
attender at Dolmetsch's concerts. Knowing what a discriminating music
critic Shaw was, and how quick to debunk anything phoney, one feels that
Dolmetsch's work must indeed have been impressive.

While the musical establishment remained massively aloof, Dolmetsch
continued with his own personal mission, the authentic interpretation of
early music on the instruments for which it was written. (Curiously, these

influential ideas about authentic performance practice, which were at first applied exclusively to early music, are now being used to re-examine the music of composers like Brahms who were living and writing when Dolmetsch was a young man.) From the beginning it was crucial to him to marry the music to the correct instruments, played according to the instructions of the period, so that while others conducted dry musicological

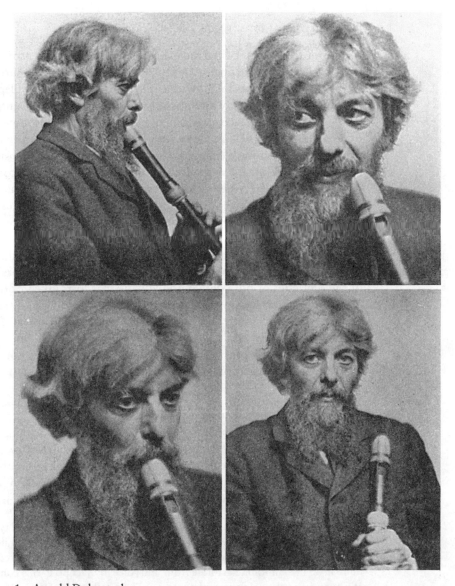

1 Arnold Dolmetsch

experiments with old instruments or played old scores on modern instruments, he brought the music to life. Dolmetsch's work created a climate of interest which fostered the growth of early music and instruments but it must be realised that the recorder was never one of his main preoccupations. It was not until 1905, when his reputation as a performer and instrument maker was well established, that he acquired his first recorder and it was fifteen years later, when he was aged sixty-two, that he first made one.

OTHER DEVELOPMENTS

Credit for the revival of the recorder has sometimes been attributed almost exclusively to England and to the Dolmetsch family in particular, but there is, in fact, clear evidence to show that the movement began independently in England and in Germany and possibly in other European countries also. As in all such cases of the development of human ideas and resources, the revival of recorder playing was an idea whose time had come and an examination of the background shows a chain of events and influences which fostered further development. While it has generally been assumed that the recorder became completely obsolete when it lost ground to the transverse flute in the late eighteenth century, there is now a body of opinion which suggests that it did survive, like an endangered species, in various isolated pockets. Hermann Moeck (1978), in his account of the recorder revival in Germany, cites several examples from the nineteenth century which lend weight to this argument. He also holds that while recorders ceased to be made and makers' knowledge of the subtleties of bore design and voicing was lost, much of the basic tradition of recorder making was preserved in the production of related instruments such as the French and English flageolets and the czakan. These instruments were widely made, sold and played in the late nineteenth century, although as popular instruments for amateurs they were not part of any 'official' musical tradition.

Before the revival really began to gain ground there were a number of fairly isolated instances of recorders being played. These are documented by Hunt (1977), Moeck (1978) and Haskell (1988). The first of these was a performance by a group from the Brussels Conservatoire at the International Inventions Exhibition held in the Albert Hall galleries in South Kensington, London, in 1885, of which the *Musical Times* reviewer commented:

From the point of view of abstract musical effect, the efforts of the players of course varied greatly. Some of the effects were beautiful as well as curious, while others were only curious. In the latter category must be placed the sounds produced by the eight *flauti dolci* in a Sinfonia Pastorale from 'Eurydice' by Jacopo Peri, a composer generally considered the originator of opera . . . The pupils of M. Dumon's class handled

4

them well, but the effect resembled a description of a street organ now happily but rarely heard. *(Musical Times, 1885)*

Hermann Moeck (1978) records the existence of the Bogenhausener Künstlerkapelle (Bogenhausen Artists' Band), a group of seven friends, mainly amateur musicians, who first formed themselves into a band in the 1890s to play, on original instruments, Handel, Scarlatti, Gluck, Mozart, etc. In the years up to the outbreak of the Second World War, the 'Bogenhausen-ers' became an established part of the musical scene in Munich, playing for civic receptions and festivities and broadcasting. In 1925 they were 'legit-imised' to the extent of being invited to perform at the Munich Bach Festival.

In Britain during the 1890s and early 1900s, the research and lectures of Canon Francis Galpin, Dr Joseph Cox Bridge and Christopher Welch drew some attention to the recorder in musical circles but very little was then known about the manner of playing the instrument or the music written for it. Indeed, in 1901, when Dr Bridge gave a lecture and demonstration of the four recorders by Bressan which are now housed in the Grosvenor Museum in Chester, he and his fellow performers were so baffled by the function of the thumb-holes that they covered them with stamp paper and used whistle fingering (Hunt 1977, 129).

REDISCOVERY OF RECORDER MAKING

As interest began to grow in all early instruments, it began to be apparent that there were not enough original instruments available in playing condition to meet the demands of those who wished to have them. The question of redis-covering the skills to make them began to arise and here again it is now clear that this was a problem addressed at much the same time in several countries, most notably England and Germany. Arnold Dolmetsch undoubtedly led the field in instrument making and performance at the turn of the century. His lecture-recitals were by then taking him and his family on tour in Britain and on the Continent, as well as to America, and he was fully engaged in making early instruments of all kinds when, in 1905, he acquired an early-eighteenth-century boxwood and ivory recorder by Bressan at a Sotheby's sale. He had not, at this stage, investigated any of the early wind instruments, but a sea voyage to America gave him the time to teach himself to play it using an eighteenth-century tutor book. From then on he used it regularly in his con-certs (Campbell 1975, 164–6). The famous story of the loss of this recorder at Waterloo Station in 1919 by the seven-year-old Carl Dolmetsch is well known* (Campbell 1975, 208–9). It precipitated Arnold's far-reaching

---

* There is an apparent anomaly of dates here. The recorder was lost, according to Arnold Dolmetsch's diaries, on 30 April 1919. Carl Dolmetsch was born on 23 August 1911 and thus was indeed aged seven at the time, as he remembers. From this has arisen a widespread error

decision to attempt to add a recorder to the other instruments he had made, since he found he now could not do without it in his concerts. This proved to be by no means easy, but after a succession of experiments and failures Dolmetsch finally succeeded in making a recorder that satisfied him and the first models went on sale in 1920. Among the purchasers at this early stage were George Bernard Shaw; Judith Masefield, daughter of the poet John Masefield; the cartoonist Edmund X. Kapp and Sir Bernard Darwin, son of Charles Darwin (Carl Dolmetsch, personal communication).

In Europe, Willibald Gurlitt (1889–1963) was one of the first musicians to take a practical interest in early music and to realise the importance of playing it on the appropriate instruments and not their modern equivalents. In 1920 and 1921 he began to lecture at the University of Freiburg on 'Instruments and instrumental music in the Baroque period' and to give a seminar on Michael Praetorius's *Syntagma Musicum*. As well as commissioning a reconstruction of a 'Praetorius organ' from the firm of Walcker and Co. of Ludwigsburg (Haskell 1988, 57), he borrowed the famous set of Kynseker recorders from the Germanisches Museum in Nuremberg and had copies of five of them made by the same firm (Moeck 1978). Knowing nothing of Arnold Dolmetsch, who was at very much the same time making his first recorder, he and his students used them to play seventeenth-century consort music. Another musicologist, Werner Danckerts (1900–70), also had copies made of the Kynseker instruments by the Nuremberg woodwind maker, Georg Graessel, in 1921. Subsequent copies made at his request were played at lecture-recitals in various parts of Germany in the 1920s (Moeck 1978). The Nuremberg instruments were not comparable in quality and preservation with Dolmetsch's Bressan, however, so copying them proved difficult and the end result was not very successful.

One of the first recorder players of note in Germany at this time was Gustav Scheck (1901–84). He began playing recorder and baroque flute in the 1920s, having studied under Gurlitt in Freiburg. In 1930 he began what became a famous partnership with August Wenzinger, the viola da gamba player, and Fritz Neumeyer, the harpsichordist, which pioneered the performance of old music on authentic instruments at low pitch. In 1934 Scheck was appointed to the staff of the Berlin Hochschule für Musik; Hindemith was at that time professor of composition there and had two years earlier composed his *Trio* for recorders. As we shall see, many of Hindemith's composition students later went on to write for recorders. Between them, Scheck and Gurlitt trained many of the next generation of recorder players, the pioneers of the early music movement and, in particular, of the twentieth-century repertoire

(made even in Dolmetsch publicity literature) that the recorder was lost in 1918 and the first 'new' recorder was made in 1919, a year earlier than the real sequence of events.

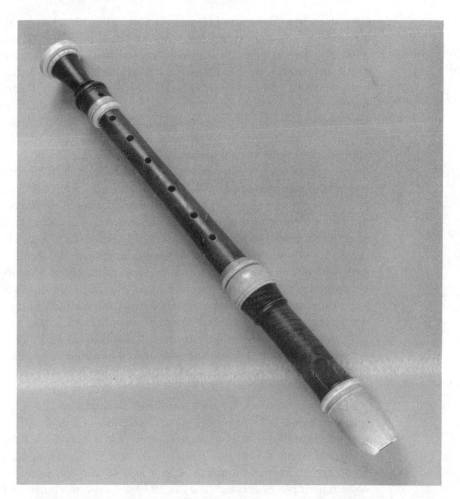

2 The recorder that started it all. Arnold Dolmetsch's boxwood and ivory treble, made by Bressan in London, c. 1700

for the recorder. Among their pupils were the player and teacher Ferdinand Conrad; the recorder maker Hans-Conrad Fehr; the musicologists and teachers Linde Höffer von Winterfeld and Hildemarie Peter; and the player, composer and teacher Hans-Martin Linde. They can thus be said to have initiated the serious study of the recorder and its music, not just in Germany, but in many other parts of Europe where their pupils subsequently worked.

MASS-PRODUCTION

In 1920, having developed a successful design for an alto recorder, Arnold Dolmetsch in England began to investigate the possibility of making the other sizes also and at the second Haslemere Festival in 1926 he was able to unveil a consort of soprano, two altos, tenor and bass recorders (Campbell 1975, 219–20). These were fine instruments which sold well to professional musicians but they were expensive and it is possible that the instrument might have remained exclusively in the rarefied province of 'serious' early music but for the growth of amateur and school recorder playing on the Continent, particularly in Germany, in the 1920s and 1930s. The popularising force in Germany was the Youth Movement, an umbrella name which came to be applied to several organisations such as the *Hausmusik* movement, the *Singbewegung* and the *Wandervögel*, all of which aimed to promote domestic and school music-making. The Youth Movement later became tainted with Nazism but in its beginnings in the first two decades of the twentieth century until Nazi ideology prevailed, it was an innocent manifestation of a desire to reject the artificial values of an increasingly mechanical age. The leaders of the Youth Movement, like those of the Arts and Crafts Movement in England with whom Dolmetsch was acquainted and with whose philosophy he was very much in tune, wanted to return to simple spiritual values and seek truth and beauty in all aspects of everyday life. Music was an important tool and the appeal of the recorder and other members of the pipe family was immediate. Repertoire mainly consisted of folksongs and dance music, but increasingly close links with the early music movement also had their effect and during the thirties many works in the *Hausmusik* genre made their appearance.

Similar movements in other European countries in the 1930s had very much the same 'back to nature' aims. The Pipers' Guild in Britain promoted the making and playing of bamboo pipes. Their president, Ralph Vaughan Williams, wrote a very fine *Suite for Pipes* (1939), now usually played on recorders. In France the bamboo pipe movement was popular also and a collection of pieces entitled *Pipeaux 1934* was commissioned by Louise Dyer from composers such as Milhaud, Roussel, Auric, Ibert and Poulenc. Similar attempts were made elsewhere in Europe to introduce the various forms of six-holed pipe. Ultimately the recorder prevailed, presumably because it was the most musically satisfactory member of the family.

If Arnold Dolmetsch is credited with the revival of recorder making in England, Peter Harlan (1898–1966) is generally regarded as his counterpart in Germany. Harlan was a violin maker who set up his own musical instruments business in Markneukirchen in the Vogtland region in 1921. Over the years he has acquired a slightly dubious reputation as the person responsible for devising the so-called 'German', as opposed to baroque or English, fingering for the recorder, but it is the present writer's opinion that without Harlan's role in ensuring a supply of instruments for the growing recorder movement in Germany in the 1920s and 1930s, instruments which began to be imported into England in the late 1930s, the present picture of recorder playing world-wide would look very different indeed. When Fritz Jöde, one of the leaders of the Youth Movement, wanted a supply of cheap recorders, Harlan, who had been a member of the *Wandervögel* in his youth, was willing to do what he could to assist and also, of course, saw an excellent business opportunity. It has always been believed (Hunt 1977, 130–1) that Harlan's recorders were bad copies of a Dolmetsch instrument which he purchased on a visit to the first Haslemere Festival in 1925. Moeck (1978), however, basing his information on conversations with Harlan after the Second World War, refutes this, stating that Harlan never actually made recorders himself and had already commissioned a copy of one of the instruments in the Staatliche Hochschule für Musik, Berlin, as the basis for his first design. This was then executed by a workshop in the Vogtland region and, according to Moeck, went on sale in early summer 1926. However, he certainly did order a recorder on his visit to Haslemere and when it was sent to him in due course he studied it closely.

Harlan, therefore, acted as the middleman, adjusting his designs to meet the requirements of his clients from the Youth Movement and farming the orders for low-priced, mass-produced recorders out to a number of instrument-making firms in the Vogtland region, an area long established as a centre for the woodwind-making industry. Recorders quickly began to be made by, or under the aegis of, other firms. Among these were such well known names as Bärenreiter, Herwig, Heinrich, Adler, Mollenhauer, Nagel and Moeck, many of them still in production today.

DESIGN PROBLEMS

Historical accuracy was not a priority with Harlan and he saw no reason why the recorder should not be 'improved' to suit his purposes. This attitude, which now seems so ill-advised, must be seen in the context of its time. The quest for authenticity is a phenomenon of the second half of the twentieth century rather than of the first and Harlan was not the only one, either then or since, to advocate modifications to the recorder which are now seen as inappropriate. His 'German' fingering system was an attempt to simplify the forked fingerings that are necessary on baroque recorders. The result was that while his recorders could be played in tune in the lower octave of the home key, they were out of tune in the higher octave and in other keys. The system, therefore, presupposes that the instrument is used only to play diatonic music with a range of one and a half octaves or so in the home key. Unfortunately, this fingering system, which actually does very little to alleviate the struggles of the beginner, also has regrettable consequences for the sound quality, a result of the change in bore shape which accompanies it. The end result is an inadequate instrument which lends itself to low standards of playing and musicianship. These cheap mass-produced instruments are, unfortunately, still being made.

Another controversial question for the German recorder makers in the late 1920s and early 1930s was that of tuning. Surviving original instruments were made, as we know, in various historical low or high pitches which might be a semitone or more different from modern pitch. Harlan and his colleagues did not always fully understand this, though they were aware of it, and early copies of recorders were made in almost every possible key (Moeck 1978). After a certain amount of confusion, recorder consorts in A and D, and C and F became accepted as the norm and eventually, because it was appropriate for the performance of early music, the C/F tuning which is nowadays regarded as standard, won the day.

2   The contemporary recorder

During the 1930s and 1940s, Great Britain, Germany and the Netherlands became, and to a great extent still are, the main centres of recorder playing. In Britain there was a growing number of amateur recorder players and the need for a reasonably-priced instrument of more modest make than the individually-crafted Dolmetsch recorders became obvious to Edgar Hunt (b. 1909), a pioneer of the English revival. He persuaded the German firm of Herwig, who had been making recorders for Harlan, to modify their existing design and produce low-price recorders with the correct or 'English' fingering for the British market (Hunt 1977, 135). It is in large part due to Edgar Hunt's good offices in this respect that suitable instruments then became available to schools and amateur players, thereby encouraging the spread of recorder playing. The formation in 1937 of the Society of Recorder Players (SRP) by Edgar Hunt and Carl Dolmetsch, together with Max and Stephanie Champion, provided an invaluable framework for the exchange of information about the instrument and its music, a function it continues to fulfil to the present day. Far from being interrupted by the Second World War, the revival of the recorder continued apace both in Britain and on the Continent and also in the United States. The portability, simplicity and cheapness of the instrument made it ideal under difficult wartime conditions and many schools adopted it as a means of introducing children to music, influenced by the work of such pioneering music educators as Carl Orff and Zoltán Kodály. At the opening ceremony of the 1936 Olympic Games in Berlin, a gymnastic display was accompanied by children playing music for recorders and other instruments specially composed for the occasion by Orff (Haskell 1988, 64).

In the 1940s and 1950s, the music available for the recorder consisted largely of rediscovered seventeenth- and eighteenth-century solo and consort music, together with arrangements of folksong material and a quantity of new compositions which may conveniently be designated by the German term, *Spielmusik*, that is, music composed with the aim of providing simple, pleasant material for the amateur. As interest in the recorder spread, new works of a more serious musical content began to appear and by the mid- to late 1950s the foundations of our modern repertoire had been laid. In the 1960s the recorder entered an entirely new phase of development. Composers of the previous decade had treated it as a melody instrument pure and simple, with little to differentiate it from the flute or any of the other woodwinds, and the new compositions of that period tended to be largely conventional in style. Now, however, a number of factors coincided to produce a radical reappraisal of the instrument and to take it out of what Gerhard Braun has referred to as the 'ghetto of the neo-baroque' (Braun 1978, 12).

The 1960s, which were inherently years of change and ferment, saw a great upsurge of interest in early music of all kinds and the corresponding increase in scholarly research into early instruments produced a good deal of new information about recorder technique and performance practice. This in turn led to a rise in playing standards as it became clear that the recorder had a specific technique of its own, distinct from that of any other woodwind instrument.

This development in understanding of the recorder came at a good time. Instrumental technique in general was being explored as players and composers searched for new sounds and timbres. The theatrical dimension of musical performance gained in importance and some composers took every opportunity to jolt audiences out of what they saw as their passive complacency. It was in this climate that the search for a twentieth-century idiom for the recorder began. Audiences for recorder music were growing rapidly and the new generation of players led by Frans Brüggen in the Netherlands and Michael Vetter in Germany was eager to have contemporary works to play. The challenge of finding a voice for the recorder in new music was stimulating to composers and performers alike, all the more so because the recorder had missed out on the important musical developments of the nineteenth century and was, therefore, coming fresh from the Baroque into twentieth-century music without any overlay of nineteenth-century tradition. This combination of circumstances led to an upsurge of compositional activity in the 1960s and produced many of the most important and innovative recorder works yet written in the twentieth century.

PERSONALITIES

Carl Dolmetsch

The development of the recorder repertoire over the last three decades has largely been the result of the efforts of a few dedicated musicians whose innovative ideas have proved to be catalysts for change. Dr Carl Dolmetsch has been a pillar of the British recorder revival for many years and has continued his father's pioneering work both in instrument making and through

12

his worldwide lecture and recital tours in which he is accompanied by members of his family. It is largely due to his influence as a performer, maker and promoter of recorders and recorder playing that many new works have been written. Much of the British recorder music written since the Second World War has been commissioned by Dolmetsch, who has made a point of playing at least one new work by a British composer at each of his annual London recitals at the Wigmore Hall. These were begun in 1939 and the programme on that occasion contained a composition of his own, *Theme and Variations* for recorder and piano, which was probably one of the first performances in Britain of a modern recorder work. In the same year another historic event took place, the performance of a whole programme of modern recorder music played by Edgar Hunt, Carl Dolmetsch and other members of the Dolmetsch family. Among the works performed were sonatinas specially commissioned from Stanley Bate, Lennox Berkeley, Christian Darnton and Peter Pope, as well as the recorder trio from Hindemith's *Plöner Musiktag*.

The list of composers who have written works for Dolmetsch is impressive. To date, he has given the first performance of some fifty works by British composers, the vast majority commissioned by him. Among those represented are Cyril Scott, Edmund Rubbra, Arnold Cooke, Gordon Jacob, Robert Simpson, Alun Hoddinott, Colin Hand, Alan Ridout, William Mathias, Nicholas Maw and Michael Berkeley. Dolmetsch has made a further important contribution in the sphere of teaching. The annual Dolmetsch Summer School and Haslemere Festival draw large attendances. His role as a founder member and first musical director of the Society of Recorder Players has already been mentioned.

Frans Brüggen

Frans Brüggen (b. 1934) is the only recorder player so far to have achieved a truly international reputation on a par with that of instrumentalists in other fields and he is very much a leading figure in the twentieth-century recorder movement. Having studied with Kees Otten and Joannes Collette in the Netherlands, Brüggen began his performing career in the mid-1950s and went on to develop his own very individual style of playing, based on his researches into renaissance and baroque performance practice as well as on his study of the structure and playing qualities of surviving early recorders. Brüggen's playing, which has been both extensively imitated and extensively criticised, is very expressive and flexible and technically very accomplished. It has been the main influence in the development of what is now regarded as the 'Dutch school' of playing, in which most of today's top players and teachers have been trained.

When he first began to play it was immediately clear to Brüggen that the limited early repertoire must be supplemented by good new composition. As

13

a result of his efforts in this direction, some of the most important contemporary works for recorder were written for him, among them such landmarks in the modern repertoire as *Gesti* by Luciano Berio and *Fragmente* by Makoto Shinohara. As a result of his performing and teaching activities, playing standards in the Netherlands, and increasingly elsewhere, have risen considerably and it is now accepted among aspiring young professional players that the recorder requires the same intensive and methodical study as any other instrument. It has even been said that present-day technical accomplishment in recorder playing has now surpassed anything achieved in the renaissance and baroque periods.

Musicians of Brüggen's calibre generally express themselves through a more mainstream instrument and it is very fortunate for the recorder that he provided a role-model for other players and an inspiration to composers at just the right point in the revival. For Brüggen, the attraction of the instrument was immediate. When he first encountered the recorder he remembers thinking, 'I want to do this for the rest of my life', and his whole face still lights up when he recounts this early reaction. Although he also plays the baroque flute and is nowadays increasingly taken up with directing his Orchestra of the Eighteenth Century, it is clear that his love for the instrument has not diminished and it is this that has communicated itself to audiences over the years.

3 Frans Brüggen

David Munrow

David Munrow (1942–76) had little direct involvement in modern recorder music although a number of very worthwhile pieces were written for him. However, he did more than anyone else to bring early music to a mass audience and in so doing helped to create the conditions in which a modern

4   David Munrow

repertoire could develop. With his group, The Early Music Consort of London, Munrow toured all over the world in the early 1970s and undertook many radio and TV broadcasts and recordings. The success of this group in reaching new audiences was in large part due to Munrow's outstanding gift as a communicator, and as a result of his activities, many people were introduced to the recorder and to other early instruments who would otherwise not have come into contact with them.

Michael Vetter

The German recorder player Michael Vetter (b. 1943) made a significant contribution to the development of a new idiom for the recorder. He was encouraged in this by contacts with some of his contemporaries among the then younger generation of Dutch musicians such as Brüggen and the composers Louis Andriessen and Rob du Bois. Some of the first and most daring avant-garde works were written for him. These included Jürg Baur's *Mutazioni* and *Pezzi Uccelli*; *Spiel und Zwischenspiel* by du Bois; and *RARA* by Sylvano Bussotti. In the late 1960s Vetter's own graphic electronic compositions, *Figurationen III* and *Rezitative*, appeared.

At about this time Vetter also began to give performances on recorder of Stockhausen's improvisatory work, *Spiral* (1969), for soloist and short-wave radio receiver, thus taking the recorder out of the realm of the specialist and into the wider world of contemporary music. In 1970 he travelled to Japan as a member of the Stockhausen-Ensemble to take part in performances of this and other works at the Expo '70 World Fair in Osaka. During a long stay in Japan, Vetter further developed and added to his repertoire. Influenced by traditional music, in particular that of the shakuhachi and the Japanese Noh flute, he began to develop his improvisatory powers, incorporating techniques learnt from Japanese musicians as well as those acquired through his experience of working with Stockhausen and performing his music. He developed a recorder improvisation called *Fuenota* ('Song of the Flute') and his performance of the work in London in 1970 is still vividly remembered by those who were present. One description says that he played continuously for sixty minutes, seated cross-legged on a white rug lit by green and purple lighting, guided in his improvisations only by a small piece of paper at his feet (Clark 1971, 338).

In the 1960s Vetter's lack of any formal training either as a recorder player or as a composer caused him to be regarded in some quarters as a dilettante, in strong contrast to the ambitious professionalism of Brüggen and his disciples. As the 'enfant terrible' of the recorder world, he shocked many audiences with the outrageous theatricality of his performances but he also made an enormous contribution in developing avant-garde techniques for the recorder and in presenting an alternative to the bland and somewhat precious

16

image which was threatening to engulf the instrument as the revival gained in momentum.

In the early 1970s Vetter returned to Japan where he lived for the next twelve years, largely dropping from sight in Western musical circles. He developed his interest in philosophy and theology by studying Eastern religions such as Zen and Taoism and lived as a monk in a Buddhist monastery. Vetter has now returned to live in the West and has begun to appear on the concert platform again. In the BBC's Stockhausen Festival, 'Music and Machines', at the Barbican Centre in London in January 1985 he gave a vocal performance of *Spiral*. This extraordinary demonstration of vocal and theatrical virtuosity, evidently much influenced by Japanese traditional music, combined with his stage presence, made a considerable impact on the audience and showed clearly why his performances have always attracted so much comment and interest. He has now set up a study centre in Germany where students can come to absorb his own particular blend of Eastern philosophy and religion, music and the arts.

Hans-Martin Linde

Another figure who has made an important contribution to the growth of modern recorder music is the German recorder player and composer Hans-Martin Linde (b. 1930), who has been a member of the staff of the Schola Cantorum of Basel, Switzerland, since 1957. In Europe, Linde's influence as a player and teacher has been great and his interest in modern music and in the development of a contemporary repertoire for the recorder has been important in extending the horizons of his students beyond the confines of renaissance and baroque music and in making it a living, rather than an historic, instrument. He is also a prolific composer for recorders and since 1960 has written some two dozen works including such well-known pieces as *Music for a Bird* and *Amarilli mia Bella*, all of which make effective use of extended techniques (p. 60).

THE RECORDER WORLDWIDE

The recorder is now fully established as a popular instrument and is earning increasing respect and attention in serious music circles. It is taught in schools and conservatoires all over the world and there are few countries, however remote, without at least a nucleus of committed amateur players. In Europe, amateur and professional activities are thriving and are coordinated by recorder societies such as the Association Française pour la Flûte à Bec, the Società Italiana del Flauto Dolce and the Dutch Huismuziek Organisation, and in Britain, the Society of Recorder Players. In the Federal Republic of Germany, recorder playing is very popular and the music schools and conservatoires are producing many good players. Nevertheless, in spite of the work of dedicated players, composers and teachers such as Gerhard Braun, the recorder is still widely regarded as a school instrument and a German-fingered soprano recorder is to be found in nearly every household.

The recorder is played and taught widely in the Scandinavian countries, and Denmark, of course, is well represented internationally by Michala Petri, who has made a name principally through her many performances of baroque concertos with various well-known chamber orchestras. In Finland, Herman Rechberger's compositions and research into extended recorder techniques deserve to be better known (see Appendix). The recorder is played in educational and early music contexts in most of the countries of Eastern Europe although specific information is difficult to obtain. Much of the recent composition from these countries is pedagogical but there have been significant exceptions in such works as those of Serocki from Poland and Bozay and Dubrovay from Hungary.

The European growth of interest in the recorder as a vehicle for twentieth-century music has not been paralleled by a similar development in the United States of America, where the recorder is still regarded very much as a revived early instrument. At an amateur level enthusiasm for the recorder is enormous but there is surprisingly little serious compositional activity. A number of players such as Pete Rose and Andrew Waldo have commissioned and performed new works. Rose (b. 1942) has worked with electronics and has developed extended techniques involving circular breathing and structurally-modified recorders. After an interval of some years he is now returning to the concert platform with compositions of his own as well as works by the American composer Tui St George Tucker. Ms Tucker has been investigating modern recorder techniques for her compositions since the 1950s. The American Recorder Society, founded in 1939, provides the focus for amateur and educational recorder playing and has active chapters all over the United States and Canada. The society publishes a periodical, *The American Recorder*, and organises summer schools and graded examinations for its members. In Canada, the work of Peter Hannan is of some significance particularly in the area of electro-acoustics. The recorder is also well represented in some South American countries and likewise in South Africa.

Since the Second World War, interest in the recorder has been growing steadily in Australia and New Zealand. In both there are good composers writing for recorders: John Rimmer in New Zealand and Ros Bandt, Malcolm Tattersall and Benjamin Thorn, among many others, in Australia. Tattersall (1984; 1987) has compiled a catalogue of the most recent contemporary Australian recorder music which lists well over one hundred pieces and continues to grow. He maintains that in Australia more music has been written for recorder since 1980 than in the previous forty years. This is perhaps explained by the keen interest in school and amateur playing to

18

which is now being added a professional performing and composing dimension. There are a number of recorder societies in Australia, one of the most active of which is the Victorian Recorder Guild of Melbourne, which runs a high-profile festival every two years with participation from all the top names in the international recorder world.

Recorder playing in Japan is in a healthy state and European performers attract large audiences. There is a special sympathy for the recorder because of its likeness to the shakuhachi.

The demand for instruments and music worldwide is at present such that recorder making and the publication of recorder music from all periods now accounts for a sizeable proportion of the international music industry. Professional players tend to have their recorders specially designed and made by individual craftsmen with whom they can discuss their exact requirements beforehand, but for the less specialised the large instrument-making firms such as Dolmetsch in England, Moeck, Mollenhauer and Roessler in Germany and Küng in Switzerland have all expanded their production and added new designs. At the top of the market are the firms of von Huene and Prescott of the United States. Plastic recorders in all sizes up to and including bass are now in widespread use, made by such firms as Aulos, Yamaha and Zen-On in Japan and Dolmetsch and Schott in England. The design of these recorders is very much better than it used to be and, although no substitute for wood, a good plastic instrument is a very acceptable starting point for a beginner.

There can be few music publishing houses which do not include recorder music in their catalogues and some publishers, such as Schott and Co. of London and Mainz, and Moeck Verlag of Celle in the Federal Republic of Germany specialise in it. In the catalogues of these two firms alone may be found much of the recorder music written in the twentieth century. Series such as Schott's Recorder Library and Recorder Ensemble, as well as the Society of Recorder Players Series which they also published, introduced some of the earliest modern compositions. In Germany, the same function was performed by the Moeck series Zeitschrift für Spielmusik, Der Bläserchor and Das Blockflöten-Repertoire.

3 The recorder

The recorder belongs to one of the oldest of the musical instrument families, the whistle flutes. Archaeological evidence traces members of this family back into prehistory and simple pipes made of cane, bamboo, bone or wood are common to so many folk cultures that it seems that the fascination with the sounds to be found in them must be as old as mankind itself.

It seems certain that the recorder developed from the whistle-type folk pipe which was common in European and other folk cultures from a very early date but there is little evidence at present to indicate at what time the transition from this to the recorder proper began. The earliest surviving instrument to be clearly identified as a recorder was found in the moat of a large fortified house in Dordrecht, Holland, and is now in the Gemeentemuseum in The Hague. This instrument has not been dated precisely but since it is known that the house was occupied between 1335 and 1418 only, a late-fourteenth- or early-fifteenth-century date is probable (Weber 1976). Evidence from painting, sculpture and literature suggests an even earlier origin. For instance, woodcarvings of musical instruments on a choir-stall in the thirteenth-century cathedral at Chichester in England are said to represent recorders (Hunt 1977, 9).

DERIVATION OF THE NAME

The origin of the English name 'recorder' has been the subject of much scholarly discussion (Welch 1911; Trowell 1957; Higbee 1965). The most widely favoured derivations are from the obsolete verb 'to record', meaning to warble or sing like a bird; from the Latin *recordari*, to be mindful of or to recollect; or from the Italian *ricordo*, a keepsake or remembrance. In Europe the recorder has had many names at various times in its history, most of them referring to the construction or sound of the instrument and including the 'flute' designation; examples are the German name *Schnabelflöte* and the French *Flûte à neuf trous*. Nowadays the recorder is known in Germany as *Blockflöte*, in Italy as *flauto dolce* or *flauto diritto*, in France as *flûte à bec* and

20

in the Netherlands as *blokfluit*. Edgar Hunt (1977, 2–7) gives a full account of these names and their derivations.

DESCRIPTION OF THE INSTRUMENT

Musical sound is produced from a recorder by blowing through a whistle-type mouthpiece set in one end of a vertically-held pipe (Fig. 1). The pipe, typically made of wood, is pierced by a number of holes of which the thumb hole at the back and the first three finger-holes are covered by the thumb and fingers of the left hand and the remaining four holes by the fingers of the right

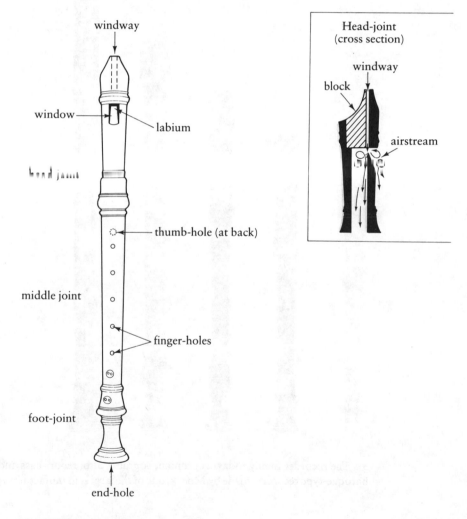

Fig. 1 The parts of a recorder

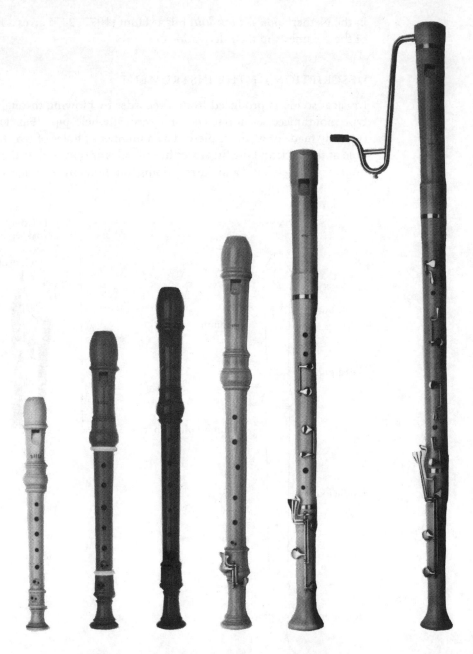

5   The recorder family today: sopranino, soprano, alto, tenor, bass and great bass.
Baroque-type recorders made by Moeck, one of the largest manufacturers of recorders

hand. The recorder is distinguished from the other whistle flutes by the presence of this thumb-hole, which when 'vented' or partially opened assists the instrument to overblow at the octave and serves the same function as the speaker key in other woodwinds. Another distinguishing feature is the shape of the bore which is characteristically conical, tapering towards the foot.

Recorders are made in different sizes (Plate 5), the pitch being determined by the length of vibrating air-column they can contain. Nowadays the four principal members of the family are the soprano, alto, tenor and bass recorders.* Of these four, the most important today is the alto recorder. Its physical dimensions are the most suited to the inherent design of the instrument in terms of tone quality and projection and it is, therefore, the most suitable solo instrument. The soprano, because of its small size, is the instrument most beginners are taught first and largely because of this it has achieved a degree of prominence in the recorder family in recent times that it did not possess in the past. The tenor and bass are used mainly in recorder consorts, although both are now proving attractive to contemporary composers as solo instruments and have been used in a number of avant-garde works. At either extreme of the range covered by these four recorders are the sopranino at the upper end and the great bass and contrabass at the lower end. These instruments lend themselves to specialised roles in solo and consort music where their particular qualities of timbre and handling are very useful. The contrabass, for instance, has recently found a new niche in electronic music.

The recorder is not a transposing instrument and players must, therefore, learn to apply the basic fingering sequence, which remains the same on all recorders, to different keys. Soprano, tenor and great bass recorders are built in the key of C, while sopranino, alto, bass and contrabass are built in the key of F. During the renaissance and baroque periods recorders were also made in keys other than these. Altos in G and D, sopranos in D and basses in G were evidently quite widely played, judging from the instruments surviving in museum collections, and these too are now proving useful in contemporary music (Fig. 2). Although there are, of course, differences in response between members of the recorder family, they are not so great as to preclude proficient players from moving freely from one to another. This is quite an important factor to take into account in considering the present popularity of the recorder. The opportunity to play, not just a single instrument but four or more, together with the chance to play all the different voices in a consort, attracts many players. Composers are similarly attracted by the possibilities of a group of instruments with the same technique and basic sound, but with differing characteristics of tone and timbre and where players experience little difficulty in changing instruments in the course of a work.

---

* The nomenclature *soprano* and *alto* is used here in preference to *descant* and *treble*. The latter is a purely English usage while the former is international and unambiguous.

Garkleinflötlein   *c'''–f''''*

Sopranino   *f''–g''''*

Soprano in D (sixth flute)   *d''–e''''*

Soprano (descant)   *c''–d''''*

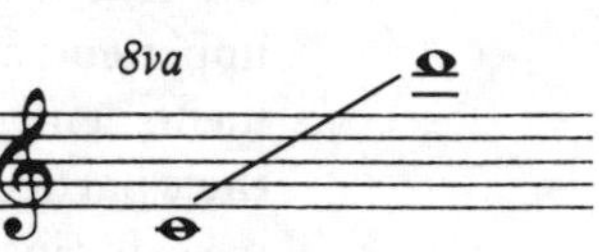

Alto in G   *g'–a'''*

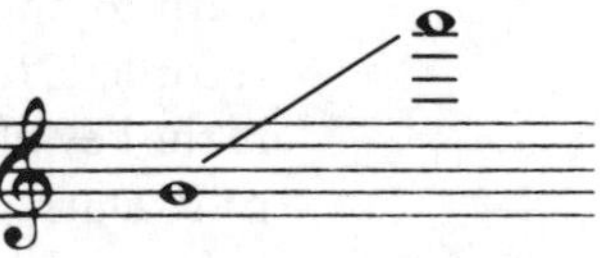

Alto (treble)   *f'–g'''*

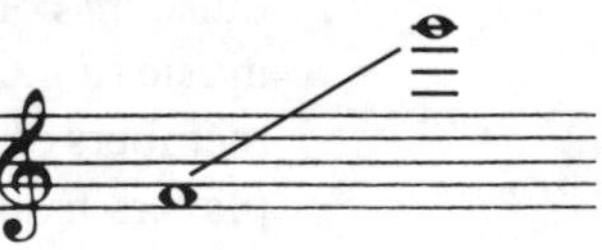

Alto in D (voice flute)   *d'–e'''*

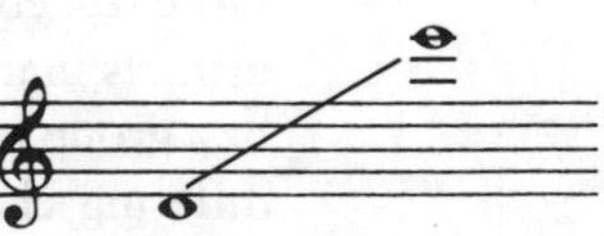

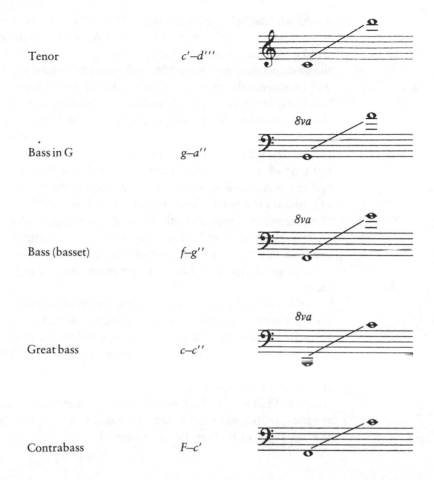

Tenor	c'–d'''
Bass in G	g–a''
Bass (basset)	f–g''
Great bass	c–c''
Contrabass	F–c'

Fig. 2 The recorder family: names, normal ranges and written pitches

MUSICAL CHARACTERISTICS

When a comparison is required to describe the sound of the recorder, the flute is the instrument which is almost invariably selected. This has inevitably led to some quite widespread misconceptions about what is desirable in recorder playing, since there is little real similarity between the instruments. Although belonging to the same class of woodwind instruments, the method of sound production in the transverse flute differs from that of the recorder in several significant ways, the most important being the formation of the airstream which produces the sound. In flute playing, the airstream is shaped by the player's embouchure and infinite variations of tone and intonation may be obtained by fine adjustment of the distance and the angle between the player's mouth and the lip of the instrument. The recorder player has no such control, since the shape of the airstream is predetermined by the dimensions of the windway. Changes in the velocity of the airstream which, by manipulation of the embouchure, may be used to enhance and colour the timbre of the flute will produce only an unacceptable sense of out-of-tuneness in the recorder unless used with great care. This direct relationship between tone-quality and the velocity of the airstream (and hence the pitch) is one of the reasons why vibrato needs to be used with particular discrimination by the recorder player. The sort of constant and fairly broad vibrato which is such an essential part of the technique of the orchestral woodwinds tends to produce a rather tense, out-of-tune effect when applied to the recorder. Clear and varied articulation is a particularly important part of recorder technique, as it is by this means more than any other that the player gives shape and momentum to the phrases. Good breath-support is an essential element in tone-production because a hard, forced tone is as undesirable as a weak, unsupported one. A fluent and facile finger technique is another obvious requirement.

In the hands of a good player, the characteristically light, open sound of the recorder is capable of great subtlety of expression, but it is true to say that the recorder is not as flexible in tone and dynamic range as the flute or the other woodwinds, nor does it have the same carrying power. The attitude of contemporary composers and players to the recorder is very largely determined by whether they regard these features in a negative or a positive light, that is to say, as limitations which put the instrument at a disadvantage or as characteristic qualities to be exploited in a musical way. It hardly needs to be said that the latter attitude is the more fruitful.

MATERIAL

The traditional material for making recorders is a well-seasoned hardwood because it can be bored and turned and its density and close grain resist the effects of moisture and changes in temperature. Many surviving seventeenth- and eighteenth-century recorders are made of boxwood and, although it is becoming increasingly difficult to obtain, present-day makers continue to use this wood. Instruments are now also made of tropical hardwoods such as the various rosewoods (dalbergia), of which African blackwood is a variety often used. Pear and maple are also used in the less expensive mass-produced sector of the market. Some eighteenth-century recorders were made of ivory, many of them elaborately carved. A few of today's top performers own fine modern recorders made from pieces of old ivory.

26

ACOUSTICS

The recorder is a member of the flute family, a large group of instruments distinguished by its characteristic method of sound production in which a jet of air is directed against the side of a lateral hole in the body of the instrument. In the case of the recorder this jet of air is directed through a fixed channel or 'windway' onto the labium or cut edge, in contrast to the transverse flute where the shape of the airstream is formed by the player's lips or 'embouchure'. Bate (1979, 2) refers to the flute family as 'air-reed' instruments because the jet of air from the player's lips corresponds to the reed of other woodwinds as a means of sound production. This term leads to a useful descriptive subdivision into 'free air-reed' instruments (such as the flute) and 'confined air-reed' instruments (such as the recorder).

The recorder functions acoustically in the manner of a cylinder open at both ends: that is to say, airwaves within the instrument are formed in the simplest mode of vibration. There is an antinode, or point of maximum displacement of air particles, at each end of the cylinder and a node, or a point of minimum displacement of air particles, in the middle. Sound is produced when air, passing through the instrument at an appropriate velocity, strikes the labium (lip) and sets up edge-tones or eddies of compression (see Fig. 1, p. 21) which are in turn communicated to the air column contained within the body of the instrument. The relationship between the dimensions of the windway and lip and their positioning relative to one another (known as the 'voicing') are critical and require the greatest skill and finesse in the making of a good instrument. Acoustically, this mouthpiece area is called the 'generator' because it generates the sound; the main body of the instrument is called the 'resonator' because it determines and stabilises the pitch. Neither can function without the other.

Like other woodwind instruments the recorder operates by offering a range of fundamental tones obtained by opening finger-holes placed at intervals along the length of the pipe. By this means the first seven diatonic notes of the range are obtained. The notes of the second octave are produced by overblowing the fundamentals in such a way as to produce the second harmonic (the fundamental being the first harmonic). In order to assist in sounding the second harmonic the tube is 'vented' by partially opening the thumb-hole. This encourages the formation of an antinode at this point. The recorder is the only one of the confined air-reed instruments which has such a vent-hole. Because the position of the thumb-hole has to be a compromise (ideally there should be a vent-hole especially placed for every note in the second octave) and because the tuning of these harmonics does not correspond with the tempered system, some adjustment of fingering and of the degree of venting is necessary to bring the notes of the second octave into tune and this is the origin of the system of cross-fingering which enables recorder players to obtain a full chromatic range without resorting to keys. Further overblowing and an appropriate thumb-hole aperture will produce some, but not all, of the notes of the third octave.

Acousticians are divided in their opinions as to what, if any, influence the material from which the tube is made has on the timbre, but most would agree that the material is of less importance than the relationship of the internal dimensions. As in any woodwind instrument, each note of the recorder is composed of a fundamental tone accompanied by a group of upper harmonics; the number and composition of this collection of harmonics is responsible for the characteristic timbre of the instrument and is determined largely by the shape of the bore. Recorders have relatively few upper harmonics and a recorder note can be acoustically very pure, which makes it an interesting instrument to use in electro-acoustic music. The paucity of upper harmonics may also explain why, although they are high-pitched, recorders do not sound shrill and listeners are sometimes deceived into thinking that the notes are sounding an octave below their actual pitch, a phenomenon noted by Praetorius in 1619 in his *Syntagma Musicum*. Thus the normal notes of the recorder (or of any instrument) are not normally the product of a single wave-formation but of a series of simultaneous wave formations or oscillations of different frequencies. This explains the availability of multiphonics or chords as an extension of recorder technique, since as long as the harmonics are in some way related (i.e. members of the same harmonic series), they are categorised by the brain as single notes, but when there is no direct harmonic relationship between them, what is heard is a group of discrete pitches which may appear to be unrelated even to the point of extreme dissonance.

RECORDER DESIGN

The evolution of recorder design since the sixteenth century, and not least in our own day, has had a considerable bearing on the sound of the instrument and on its potential as an interpretative vehicle. A consideration of the changes that have taken place in the making of recorders over the centuries provides a useful background for the evaluation of the instrument in the twentieth century.

The renaissance recorder was a simple instrument made in one or two pieces with a wide bore shaped like an inverted cone and sometimes with a slight flare in the bore towards the foot (Plate 6). The mouthpiece had a short, stubby 'beak', and the finger-holes tended to be larger than on later recorders and were placed in a straight line, except for the lowest hole, which was offset. At this period, recorders were played with either hand uppermost and where a key was required on the larger recorders, it was made with a 'swallow-tail' extension so that it could be operated by the little finger of

6 A full consort of renaissance recorders from contrabass to soprano. Modern replicas made by Adrian Brown

either hand. The tone of these early recorders tended to be more open and powerful than that of the baroque recorder and the lower notes were particularly powerful, a consequence of the construction of the bore. Evidence from contemporary literature as well as from the study of surviving instruments indicates that the compass may have been larger than that considered normal in the Baroque. In his treatise *Opera intitulata Fontegara*, published in Venice in 1535, Sylvestro Ganassi gives fingerings for the recorder spanning a range of two octaves and a sixth. The text of this work also implies a high level of virtuosity at this time, at least among Italian recorder players.

There was little change in recorder design during the sixteenth and early seventeenth centuries, but in the late seventeenth century, a number of very important structural alterations were made. Many of these are attributed to the Hotteterre family of instrument makers, who had their workshops in the village of La Couture-Boussey, about 100 kilometres from Paris. This family made innovations in all the woodwind instruments over a period of some thirty years, innovations which resulted in the transformation of the shawm into the oboe, the curtal into the bassoon and the keyless cylindrical flute into the one-keyed cylindro-conical flute. As far as the recorder is concerned, by the beginning of the eighteenth century when Jacques Hotteterre le Romain (1680–1761) published his treatise on flute, recorder and oboe technique (Hotteterre 1707), it is clear that recorder design had advanced considerably.

The baroque recorder was made in three sections, allowing greater finesse in the shaping and finishing of the bore (Plate 2). The decorative bulges and rings which transformed its outward appearance disguised the necessary thickening of the walls that gave strength to the joints. The windway was narrower, offering more resistance to the air, curved in cross-section and set in a pronounced 'beak'. The bore was narrower and, from a cylindrical head-piece, tapered considerably towards the foot. Studies of surviving baroque instruments in museum collections show that the shaping of the bore was rarely a simple taper and makers appear to have had their own reasons for curious variations in internal diameter which were undoubtedly deliberate. Clearly the shape and dimensions of the bore will influence the nature of the wave formations within it, as will the size and positioning of the finger-holes. It has been shown (Driscoll 1967, 109–13; Morgan 1982, 14–21), both by studying surviving instruments and by experimentation in making new ones, that even the slightest change in bore diameter has a great effect on the tone-quality and projection of individual notes by reinforcing certain harmonics and suppressing others. There are double holes on some recorders of this period, enabling the semitones of the two lowest notes to be played accurately, and the placing of these holes makes it clear that the practice of playing with the left hand uppermost had by then become almost universal. The flattening effect of the tapering bore made it possible to place the finger-holes closer together and this, as well as the altered dimensions of the bore, meant that chromatic notes could now be played satisfactorily by means of cross- and forked-fingerings. The baroque recorder has a softer and sweeter tone than its predecessors, enhanced by the mellow quality of baroque low pitch, a semitone or more below modern concert pitch. A range of two octaves and a note is generally accepted as having been the norm, with an upward extension of a fourth or so being obtainable on some instruments.

By the beginning of the eighteenth century, recorder design had reached a peak of technical achievement at the hands of such famous makers as the Hotteterres, the Stanesbys, Bressan, Denner and others. The only possible further improvements would have been to add keywork and perhaps modify the bore design as was done with other instruments in an attempt to strengthen the tone, extend the range by a few notes and simplify the fingering. Without some radical alteration to the sound-generating mechanism, however, a device that would make it possible to vary the shape of the air-stream and the distance from the end of the windway to the lip, such alterations would merely run the risk of destroying those features that characterise the instrument without significantly improving it.

The recorder fell into decline in the second half of the eighteenth century and can be said to have faded from the musical scene by the end of that period although, as we have seen, there were isolated instances of its survival into the nineteenth century. For all practical purposes, however, when the one-keyed transverse flute began to grow in popularity, the recorder began to decline. Many reasons have been given for the decline and eventual demise of the recorder and, as is usual in these cases, there is no simple answer. During the seventeenth and early eighteenth centuries, the recorder was 'the accepted flute of cultured music' (Bate 1979, 188); the transverse flute did not become popular until after it had been redesigned by the Hotteterre family and others at the turn of the century. That a similar redesigning along the lines of that suggested above did not take place in the case of the recorder was surely not because eighteenth-century makers were insufficiently inventive or skilled, as some writers have suggested (e.g. Waitzman 1967, 222–5), but because such a development had no musical or commercial relevance at the time. The transverse flute already possessed all the qualities an 'improved' recorder might have had, with the added advantage that it was new and fashionable.

The greater expressive powers of the flute also contributed to the decline of the recorder, although the very simplicity of tone which brought it into dis-favour was one of the features which appealed to players in the twentieth-century reaction against romanticism. Suffice it to say that in the orchestral and chamber music of the late eighteenth century, the flute was found to be far more satisfactory and so the recorder was eclipsed in much the same way as were the viol and lute, and somewhat later, the harpsichord.

THE CRAFT OF RECORDER MAKING

After this period of dormancy, when the first recorders began to be made in this century, it was as a result of an unselfconscious attempt to recreate a lost instrument. They were copied from the few surviving original instruments then known, assisted by descriptions in early treatises. The supreme skill and instinct of craftsmen such as Arnold Dolmetsch were an invaluable asset in this process of rediscovery.

The later course of recorder making in the twentieth century has been greatly influenced by Carl Dolmetsch. From a very young age he worked alongside his father and after Arnold's death in 1940 and the interregnum of the Second World War, he assumed control of the Dolmetsch workshops at Haslemere in Surrey. Taking the baroque recorder as his model, he developed his own theories about recorder design, based on the belief that the recorder should continue to evolve in order to meet the requirements of the twentieth century, namely, a bigger and more carrying sound, a fully chromatic upward extension of the range, and the ability to play softly or loudly without pitch alteration. His aim was to produce a recorder which could compete on equal terms with modern strings in large concert halls, playing both baroque and modern music.

To this end Carl Dolmetsch's recorders were made at modern pitch with a wide and frequently straight windway which required the player to blow a greater volume of air into the instrument at a higher velocity, thus giving these recorders a more open and penetrating tone than those of the baroque period (Plate 7). As well as this, they were usually tuned to equal temperament rather than to one of the unequally-tempered tunings used for wind instruments in the Baroque, so as to fit with the so-called 'English fingering' which Carl Dolmetsch was the first to implement. Now universal for modern-pitch recorders, this fingering employs double holes for the semitones of the lowest two notes and also alters the fingering of other notes higher in the range. English fingering is as much a compromise in its way as German fingering (p. 9), though not so unfortunate in its consequences. Neither should be confused with authentic baroque and renaissance fingerings.

The prestige of the name of Dolmetsch in the 1940s and 1950s ensured that these instruments were widely studied and imitated, especially when some of the large firms on the Continent began making recorders by mass-production methods.

In the late 1960s the scholarly research which accompanied the growing interest in early music led to a re-examination of the construction and playing qualities of early instruments. This resulted in a strong desire for authenticity in every detail among performers of renaissance and baroque music and it was at this point that recorder makers and players began to realise that the instruments then being made did not, in fact, bear a very close resemblance to surviving originals. As research and experimentation proceeded, it became clear that these early recorders differed from their modern counterparts in a number of critical details, notably the shape and dimensions of the windway, the voicing, the internal construction of the bore and, of course, the pitch.

The question of pitch is perhaps the most significant feature in distinguishing between modern and historical models. Although Arnold Dolmetsch's recorders were made at A = 415 Hz until about 1935, from that time

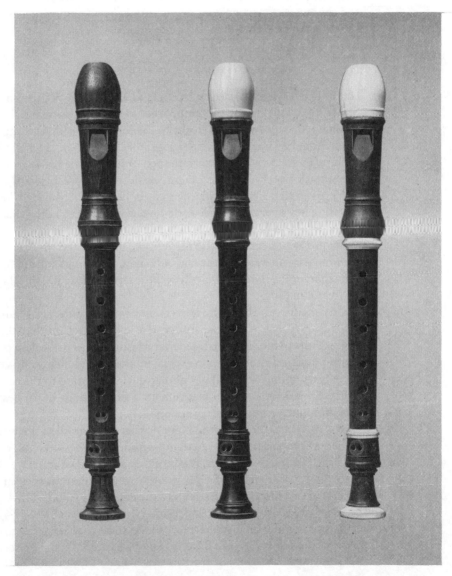

7 Dolmetsch rosewood soprano recorders

onwards most if not all recorders were made to sound at modern concert pitch of A = 440 so that they could take part in performances with piano, strings, etc. The consequent reedy quality which this gave to the tone can perhaps be evaluated fully only by contrasting it with the mellow and resonant tones of a recorder playing at baroque low pitch of A = 415 or below, or the power and brilliance of a renaissance recorder playing at one of the renaissance high pitches. The difference between the early- and the modern-pitch recorders, therefore, is as much a question of timbre as of pitch, the characteristic dimensions of the former giving a distinctive quality to the tone that is not found in modern recorders.

DESIGN INNOVATIONS

In the 1960s, Carl Dolmetsch in England and Daniel Waitzman in the United States tirelessly promoted 'improved' recorders, convinced that only by evolving in this way could the recorder survive in the modern world. Dolmetsch had already invented a number of mechanical devices such as the tone projector, a wheelbarrow-shaped object which fits over the window of the recorder and which, he claims, projects the tone forward so that it will carry over string accompaniment in a large hall; the bell key, an open-standing key operated by the little finger of the right hand which, by closing the end-hole, makes *f'''* sharp playable without resorting to the various more awkward expedients recorder players usually use; and the echo key, a closed-standing key operated by the chin which opens a small hole in the head-joint, thus sharpening the overall pitch of the instrument so that the player can blow softly but in tune.

Opponents of these 'improvements' – supporters of authenticity in recorder making – vehemently refuted any suggestion that the instrument needed improving. They claimed that it had reached its peak in the eighteenth century and that nothing present-day makers were able to do could surpass the efforts of the great makers of that day. According to the recorder maker Bruce Haynes, present-day instruments had lost many of the best qualities of the baroque recorder: 'Contemporary recorder makers are making Bowdlerised instruments which are neither truly modern nor truly Baroque; rather, a comparatively unsatisfying compromise between the two ideals . . . we have lost much of the original tone quality and character of the Baroque recorder . . . Dynamic nuances, subtlety of articulation, accurate intonation and tonal variation have all been sacrificed to such "modern" ideals as ease of playing, practicability, and structural safety' (Haynes 1968, 240). Haynes's criticisms could with justice be levelled at some makers at the time his words were written, but the situation has since changed for the better and makers are now far more aware of the principles and ethics of their craft.

Respect for the master recorder makers of the distant past has grown as research reveals the subtlety and sophistication of their methods. Indeed, it seems as if we have been merely peeling back the layers of our own ignorance. This lends weight to a growing feeling that the baroque recorder represents an evolutionary peak which is incapable of further development without the loss of the very qualities that distinguish it from its nearest relatives.

In recent years, many of the large firms have modified their designs so as to bring the instruments closer to what are now recognised to have been the intentions of the early makers, but there is still an inevitable disparity because the tooling and finish in a mass-production process are necessarily different from what can be achieved by a single craft worker making historical copies in small numbers in the workshop. Most of the more inaccurate features of mid-twentieth-century recorders have, thankfully, disappeared and instruments are no longer being made with the type of straight and very wide windway, and voicing to match, that used to be quite commonplace. Makers with whom I have discussed the question of recorder design agree that the differences between authentic replicas of historical instruments and those modern instruments which make no claim to be historically accurate are very great. Makers' catalogues nowadays show a careful distinction between recorders that are exact replicas of baroque and renaissance originals by one of the famous makers and those which are designed on baroque or renaissance principles but are not modelled on any single specific instrument. A distinction is also made in the case of those which are based on modern design

A 'MODERN' RECORDER?

Attempts have also been made to develop 'a truly modern recorder' by departing radically from pre-existing models. One such development is the metal recorder made by the firm of Hopf in the Federal Republic of Germany. The soprano is made entirely of brass, nickel-plated, and the alto is made of rosewood with a metal head-joint. Both have a system of adjustable voicing which means that the positioning of the block, height of the windway, etc. can be altered and both have a powerful carrying sound with a quality more closely resembling the metal Boehm flute than the recorder.

It has also been suggested that an instrument which is a hybrid of baroque and renaissance design might offer some useful possibilities in contemporary music. Such an instrument would have a renaissance wide bore but baroque fingering, which should give it the power of the renaissance recorder, particularly in the lower octave, and the greater range of the baroque recorder.

The Dutch maker Frans Twaalfhoven has recently begun to make recorders of an acrylic resin, a dense transparent material which is not moulded but bored and turned like wood. In other respects it is designed like a baroque recorder, with the same external outlines but a very attractive appearance because it looks as if it is made of glass. Twaalfhoven claims that it has all the sound-qualities of a good wooden instrument but with the added advantage of being much tougher. Because the material is man-made it does not absorb moisture and so can be played for many hours a day, and does not change shape with time.

Michael Barker's Interactive MIDI Performance System, the 'electrified' recorder described on p. 79, has been hailed as one of the most promising new avenues of approach but then this, unlike the others mentioned above, does not require any internal modification of the instrument itself. A modern recorder on any of the above lines, if developed successfully, could open up exciting prospects for the future. On the other hand, it must be said that the currently prevailing attitude is to accept the recorder for what it is and to look for musical rather than technological solutions.

4 Conventional recorder music and the heritage of the Baroque

The development of the contemporary repertoire is, in a sense, the story of the struggle of the recorder to be recognised as a living, growing instrument independent of its historical origins. Its identification with renaissance and baroque music meant that a compositional idiom free from the constraints of the past did not begin to develop in earnest until the 1960s and works written before that time tended to be heavily influenced by renaissance and baroque music. We can now look back over more than fifty years of steadily-increasing compositional activity and see that the repertoire contains pieces representing most of the major styles of the twentieth century, among them neo-classical works, strict and free twelve note compositions, improvised and open form works, graphic scores, music theatre pieces, minimalist compositions and works using electro-acoustics, many of which make use of extended instrumental techniques. It has proved impossible to deal in detail with all aspects of so large a body of works, consisting of so many widely-differing styles of composition, and the discussion of the repertoire has, therefore, been centred on certain broad areas covering the most significant and fruitful trends in twentieth-century recorder composition.

In the present study, 'twentieth-century' and 'modern' are used interchangeably, as they generally are in music nowadays, to describe any work written during the present century. References to the 'modern recorder repertoire' should be taken as a collective term describing all the original music (as opposed to arrangements or pedagogical material) composed for the recorder since the current revival of the instrument early in the twentieth century. The more specific term 'avant-garde recorder music' is applied here only to those works dating mainly from the 1960s and early 1970s which in their use of the instrument were the first to make innovations that went outside the historically-defined boundaries of conventional recorder technique. The term 'conventional recorder music' has been adopted, in default of a better one, to describe those works that are completely traditional in their approach to the instrument, avoiding all new playing techniques and using the recorder solely as a melody instrument. While many of the works thus referred to are, unfor-

37

tunately, somewhat trite, this is by no means true of all and the term should not be taken as one of disparagement. Examples of fine works which come under this heading are Walter Leigh's *Sonatina*, Edmund Rubbra's *Meditazioni sopra 'Coeurs Désolés'* and *Sonatina*, and the many works of Hans Ulrich Staeps, such as his ensemble pieces *Aubade und Tanz*, *Chorisches Quintett* and *Divertimento in D*.

EARLY COMPOSITIONS

The nucleus of a twentieth-century repertoire was formed with the composition in the years 1930–40 of a group of sonatinas for recorder and piano by some of the then younger generation of British composers. These were written at the instigation of Manuel Jacob, an enthusiastic recorder player himself and a student of Edgar Hunt, and the composers he commissioned were Stanley Bate, Lennox Berkeley, Christian Darnton, Peggy Glanville-Hicks, Eve Kisch, Walter Leigh, Peter Pope, Alan Rawsthorne and Franz Reizenstein. Not surprisingly, at this very early stage in the revival many of these works were overshadowed by the historical background of the recorder and were clearly influenced in their use of form and tonality by the music of the seventeenth and eighteenth centuries. In the late 1930s, however, the fact that any new works should have been contemplated for a comparatively little-known instrument shows a degree of enlightened energy on the part of those concerned that is most impressive. Although the Darnton, Kisch and Rawsthorne pieces were subsequently withdrawn by their composers, all the others were published by Schott and Co. Ltd of London in the course of the next decade or so, thus founding the modern recorder repertoire. Of this pioneering group of pieces three are still in print today: the *Partita* (1938) by Franz Reizenstein (1911–68) and the *Sonatinas* (1939 and 1940) by Walter Leigh (1905–42) and Lennox Berkeley (1903–89) respectively.

These works serve as an interesting illustration both of the style of writing for the recorder at the time and of some of the misconceptions about the instrument which, understandably enough, were then current. Most striking of these misconceptions was the tendency to regard the recorder as a sort of quieter, less flexible flute and the failure to recognise and exploit its distinctive and unique quality of sound. The perception of this quality did not come until much later, when the differences between recorder and flute technique began to be properly understood.

Of the three works mentioned above, the Berkeley is the finest and has earned a permanent place in the contemporary recorder repertoire. It is in three movements – a sonata-form first movement marked *Moderato*, a ternary second movement marked *Adagio* and a rondo-form third movement marked *Allegro moderato* – and shows Berkeley's characteristically flowing melodic lines and warm harmonic colours. The recorder part is wide-ranging and expressive and the piano part is particularly strong and sonorous, unusually so in a recorder sonata. From the point of view of the recorder player, however, there are a number of technical snags and these as well as other aspects of the work suggest that Berkeley had the sound of the flute rather than that of the recorder in mind. The dynamic markings, for instance, are in some places quite unrealistic and must be interpreted according to the spirit, rather than the letter. It is not possible to obtain a true *piano* in the upper registers of the recorder, nor is it possible to play *forte* on the lowest notes. The articulation markings indicated in the score also suggest flute rather than recorder writing and indeed the *Sonatina* is frequently played by flautists. One further difficulty arises with the use of the note *f'''* sharp. This note is particularly difficult to play on the recorder and is usually obtained by fingering *g'''* while stopping the end-hole of the recorder with the knee. Apart from the difficulty of negotiating this note at speed, the player should preferably be seated in order to be able to stop the end-hole in this manner. In general, recorder players prefer to avoid *f'''* sharp altogether and one feels that the composer may have been unaware of the difficulties associated with it.

Franz Reizenstein's *Partita* is another example of a work where the composer appears to have had the wrong sort of sound in mind. In this case it is the clarinet, rather than the recorder, which comes to mind as the most suitable vehicle for the work. The compositional style shows the influence of Reizenstein's teacher Hindemith in its thematic constructions and tonality but the choice of forms and titles for the four movements – Entrada, Sarabande, Bourrée and Jig – suggests a neo-classical influence which is borne out by the use of an English nursery rhyme song, 'Cock-a-doodle-doo, my dame has lost her shoe', as the basis for the Jig. The work as a whole does not lie well on the recorder and contains some passages which are very difficult to negotiate given the nature of recorder cross-fingerings. Dynamics are unrealistic and in general the *Partita* calls for a much brighter, stronger sound than the recorder can realistically achieve. Reizenstein himself may have felt less than satisfied with the work since he rescored it later in the same year for flute and string trio.

Walter Leigh's *Sonatina* is much more successful in its treatment of the recorder. This three-movement work achieves a satisfactory balance of sound and dynamics between recorder and piano and contains some beautiful *cantabile* passages for recorder, particularly in the second movement which is marked *Larghetto, molto tranquillo* (Ex. 1). Leigh, another student of Hindemith, uses the full chromatic compass of the recorder but has a good appreciation of the natural dynamics and tonal properties of the instrument, with the result that there are fewer problems of execution for the performer. Unfortunately, Leigh's death in action in the Second World War deprived us of any further recorder works by him, apart from a very short *Air* for alto

1   Walter Leigh, *Sonatina*, second movement

recorder and piano written in Cairo just before he was killed (Malcolm Abbs, personal communication).

Paul Hindemith

Not all composers were influenced by the early music revival, however, and one work which is significantly free from the restraints of neo-classicism is the *Trio* (1932) for recorders from the 'Plöner Musiktag' by Paul Hindemith (1895–1963). This work is remarkable not only for the very early date at which it was written but also for its serious treatment of the instruments in music that is difficult both technically and interpretatively. Hindemith was a knowledgeable and proficient player of various early instruments, including the recorder, and perhaps welcomed the chance to demonstrate the instrument in a composition of his own. The *Trio* was written for a one-day music festival held in a state high school in the town of Plön in Germany in 1932. Hindemith wrote all the music for the day's activities, which included morning 'tower music', various instrumental items in the middle of the day, an afternoon cantata and an evening concert. The recorder trio was the fifth item in this fourth part of the day, the *Abend-konzert*, and was performed by Hindemith himself together with two friends. Thus, unlike the works played earlier in the day, the *Trio* was not intended for the students but for competent adult musicians.

It is a short and concentrated work in three movements, unusual in that it ends with a *Fugato* slow movement. David Neumayer has shown in his study of the sketches and autograph score of the work (Neumayer 1976, 61–8) that Hindemith took considerable pains with the *Trio*, working and reworking some sections until they were right and not, as he sometimes did, producing the final version straight away without any revisions. The sketches show how he reworked the subject of the *Fugato* final movement, developing its structural and harmonic possibilities to the full (Ex. 2). The Scherzo also underwent several revisions before attaining its final form. The first movement remained basically the same in the autograph as in the sketches, apart from numerous variations and corrections of details. It is surprising that a small-scale work for such an unusual instrumentation should have held Hindemith's interest to this extent, but that it did so is also suggested by the fact that Arnold Cooke recalls hearing the work performed in Hindemith's composition class at the Berlin Hochschule für Musik during the period 1929–32, when Cooke was a student there (Dawney 1972, 8). Presumably Hindemith brought the *Trio* to the class for discussion. Neumayer points out that the piece is typical of Hindemith's style and compositional procedures; the tonality and forms are entirely Hindemith's own and there is no attempt to 'write down' to the recorder (Ex. 3). Apart from its skilful construction, the *Trio* shows Hindemith's usual care that all the parts should lie well for the instruments.

Hindemith scored the *Trio* for recorders in A and D, one soprano and two altos, and performed it on modern-pitch instruments of the type then being made in Germany by Harlan and others (p. 9). The general assumption has always been that this choice of instrument arose out of misunderstandings generated by Harlan's first attempts at recorder making and that only A/D sets were available at the time. Nowadays, when recorders in C/F are the

2   Paul Hindemith, *Trio*. Sketches for the *Fugato* theme. In Neumayer 1976, 61–8

3   Paul Hindemith, *Trio*, third movement, *Fugato*

norm everywhere, the Hindemith *Trio* is played in a transposed version a
minor third higher which, of course, lies better on these instruments.
Although this version, which was prepared by the late Walter Bergmann, was
authorised by the composer in 1952, there now seems to be good reason for
questioning the wisdom of such a transposition.

42

Anyone who has played the same piece of music first on a modern-pitch recorder at A = 440 and then on a low-pitch one at, say, A = 415 will have been struck by the difference in tone and response which a mere semitone produces. The reasons for this have already been discussed (p. 34). A drop in pitch of a minor third must, therefore, add far more warmth and resonance to a performance of the Hindemith *Trio*. We know that from an early stage, and certainly by 1932 when the *Trio* was composed, the German makers were aware of the difference between low and modern pitch and were making recorders in A/D, C/F and other sets of keys, so as to exploit the differences in timbre and response which they were found to offer. Such was the proliferation of tunings, indeed, that a conference of interested parties was held in 1931 to discuss the matter and the A/D tuning was preferred (although the Hitler Youth leadership later revoked this). If Hindemith, whom we know to have been unusually well-informed about the revival of baroque instruments, chose recorders in A and D in preference to recorders in C and F which would have been available to him in both modern and low pitch, we must conclude that he had good reason to do so. We should also consider whether we are not doing the work a disservice when we nowadays play it a minor third higher.

Another alteration that has sometimes been made to the original score is in the ordering of the movements. It has been said that the placing of the slow, sostenuto *Fugato* as the final movement of the work disturbs the balance, coming as it does after two fast movements, an *Allegro* and a *Vivace*, and that the *Fugato* should be the central movement of the work. Hindemith's reply to this suggestion, as given by Bergmann (1972, 17) in his commentary on the *Trio*, is that the original arrangement fitted best with the rest of the programme of which the *Trio* was a component, but that the order of movements might be reversed if the players wished. In fact, in most performances nowadays the original order is preserved since, although the *Fugato* is short, it is the most weighty and concentrated of the three movements in terms of content. The *Trio* is by no means easy to perform, either technically or interpretatively. One particular problem which always presents itself is that of tuning. The tonality of the piece is such that fingering adjustments are needed all the time, especially in the *Fugato*, to ensure that the chording is accurate. The three recorders used must be very carefully matched for timbre and volume. This is one of those few pieces with truly lasting qualities which can hold its own on any concert platform.

Unfortunately, this is Hindemith's only work for recorders and there is little else of real significance in German recorder music until the 1960s, the only exception being some compositions by Harald Genzmer (b. 1909), such as his *Sonata no. 1* (1941) for alto recorder and piano. Most German compositions of this period come into the category of *Spielmusik* and are outside the scope of this present work.

A number of composers who studied with Hindemith at the Berlin Hochschule für Musik in the decade before the Second World War went on to take a particular interest in the recorder. As well as Leigh and Reizenstein, there were Arnold Cooke and Hans Ulrich Staeps. Both these composers were strongly influenced by Hindemith in their use of structure and tonality as well as in their workmanlike approach to instrumental writing. Other students of Hindemith who later wrote recorder music include Stanley Bate, Harald Genzmer and Hans Poser, although the latter studied with him by correspondence only, during the war years. It is not possible to say to what extent these composers owe their interest in the recorder to the teaching of Hindemith, and it may be no more than coincidence that so many of the best recorder pieces of the period immediately before and after the Second World War were written by British and German composers who had studied with him in Berlin. Hindemith, however, made a point of ensuring that his composition students gained at least a basic familiarity with the music and instruments of the past, allowing them to examine and play the early instruments in the collection of the Hochschule. While it is perhaps too much to suggest that Cooke, Staeps and the others left Hindemith's class fired with enthusiasm to write contemporary music for the recorder, it does seem likely that later, when commissions appeared, they were sufficiently familiar with the instrument to be interested in writing for it.

THE 1950S AND AFTER

It was not until the 1950s that new works for recorders began to appear in any appreciable numbers. They emanated from the countries where the recorder revival was most firmly established, that is, Great Britain, Germany and the Netherlands. The output of modern recorder music from the Netherlands in the 1930s and 1940s had consisted mainly of *Spielmusik* by composers such as Jan van Dijk (b. 1918) and others. The first significant Dutch contribution to the repertoire was the *Sonata* (1967) for alto recorder and harpsichord by Henk Badings (1907–87), one of a number of fine works by this composer. This sonata, which is dedicated to Kees Otten and Jaap Spigt, then a pioneering recorder and harpsichord duo in the Netherlands, is technically and musically demanding. The composer, presumably enlightened by Otten, obviously felt no need to make any concessions to the supposed limitations of the instruments and both recorder and harpsichord parts are strong and full of character. It should be realised that at this time the harpsichord was almost as much of a *rara avis* as the recorder, and most works used piano accompaniment. The writing for harpsichord in this sonata calls for a very full and assertive sound calling to mind the sort of large, powerful instruments in use in 'pre-authenticity' days, creating an almost organ-like texture in the last movement. In the same movement there is an unusual middle section where repeated keyboard chords provide a background for a passage of fast, running semiquavers for recorder. The resemblance to a jazz 'break' is strong and this may in fact be the intention, since Kees Otten is also well known as a jazz musician.

Benjamin Britten

In Britain at this time the recorder was attracting a growing number of followers, among them Benjamin Britten (1913–76) and Peter Pears (1910–86), both good amateur players. Britten, who became president of the Society of Recorder Players in 1959, used the recorder to great effect in his children's opera *Noye's Fludde* (1958), with simple parts for a children's instrumental group and a difficult solo part, intended for a professional player, representing a dove. Britten's *Scherzo* of 1955 for four recorders was written for the amateur players of the Aldeburgh Music Club. This short fanfare-like piece with a contrasting melodic middle section calls forth exactly those characteristic qualities of timbre and precision of attack that were so rarely understood in recorder composition at that time.

The *Alpine Suite* (1955) for two soprano and one alto recorder is a charming set of short programmatic sketches portraying the events and impressions of a Swiss skiing holiday, which Britten and Pears took with their friend and

8   An open-air concert on Thorpness Meare during the 1954 Aldeburgh Festival. Front row from left: Mary Potter, to whom the *Alpine Suite* was dedicated, Benjamin Britten, Peter Pears (playing bass recorder). Imogen Holst conducts.

neighbour at Aldeburgh, the artist Mary Potter. She had the misfortune to break a leg at an early stage and was confined to the chalet so, the three having brought their recorders with them, Britten wrote the *Suite* to cheer her up. It contains everything from funicular railways to cuckoo clocks to alphorns, including a musical account of the unpredictability of the nursery slopes. It was later performed in public at the 1955 Aldeburgh Festival. Attractive and amusing as these two compositions are, they serve only to tantalise with thoughts of what a Britten concerto or sonata for recorder might have contributed to the repertoire. A suggestion has been made that Britten did, in fact, start to sketch a recorder sonata in 1939 but no supporting evidence can be found in the Aldeburgh Archive.

With one or two further exceptions, among them the *Four Inventions* (1954) for soprano and alto recorders by Michael Tippett (b. 1905), the present president of the Society of Recorder Players, the majority of British recorder works of this period reflect the continuing preoccupation of players and composers with the recorder as a revived historical instrument rather than as a living instrument with potential for further development within the context of twentieth-century music. Edmund Rubbra (1901–86) composed a total of eight works for recorder in the period between 1949 and 1977; these are a good illustration of this genre. They are fine pieces and well composed but are very much a re-creation of earlier styles and forms. Some indication of this is evident even from the titles of his compositions, *Meditazioni sopra 'Coeurs Désolés'* Op. 67 (1949) for alto recorder and harpsichord and *Fantasia on a Theme of Machaut* Op. 86 (1957) for alto recorder, string quartet and harpsichord being typical examples. Rubbra's most extended work for recorder is the *Sonatina* Op. 128 (1964) for alto recorder and harpsichord. The early music influence is clear in this work also, not only in the modal flavour of the harmony but in the choice of a sixteenth-century Spanish air as the basis for the set of variations which forms the third and final movement. Most of Rubbra's works for recorder arose out of his acquaintance with Carl Dolmetsch, who has given many performances of his work.

Arnold Cooke

Arnold Cooke (b. 1906) began to write for the recorder in the 1950s and has made a considerable contribution to the repertoire, maintaining an interest in the instrument throughout his working life. As we have seen, he was greatly influenced by Hindemith, not only in his compositional methods but in his use of instruments also. Cooke has a strong instinct for what lies well on an instrument and shows an understanding of the problems of writing for recorders which few of his contemporaries can match. All of his dozen or more recorder works are worthwhile additions to the repertoire. Some are more difficult than others but the majority are intended for competent amateurs, since Cooke, like Hindemith and Britten, believes that it is not only possible, but important to supply amateur players with good music.

The outstanding works from Cooke's output for recorder are two of the most difficult: the *Concerto* (1957) for alto recorder and string orchestra and the first *Quartett* (1970) for SATB recorders. Both are works of stature in which the recorder is accorded the status of a fully professional wind instrument. The recorder concerto is an unjustly neglected form in the modern repertoire and the Cooke *Concerto*, written for Philip Rodgers of Sheffield, is therefore all the more valuable in its relative rarity.

It is in four movements, the last of which is a set of variations on 'Prince Rupert's March' and the work as a whole is very skilfully constructed with much thematic unity. Dynamics and balance are particularly well handled, with dynamic contrast built into the structure of the music rather than superimposed by means of directions in the score. Cooke does not hesitate to use *pp* and *ff* in the recorder part, but takes care to ensure that the context is suitable and that the dynamic level of the orchestra is such as to achieve a satisfactory overall balance. By this means an abundance of contrast is created with no feeling of strain on the part of the soloist.

The *Quartett* of 1970 is certainly the best work for SATB recorders to come from a British composer of Cooke's generation. It is the most substantial of all his works for recorder and, like the *Concerto*, is not really a work for amateurs. In fact it is far more extended and weighty than the general run of pieces for recorder ensemble, the instruments being treated very much like a string quartet (Ex. 4). The sonorities of four recorders unaccompanied are

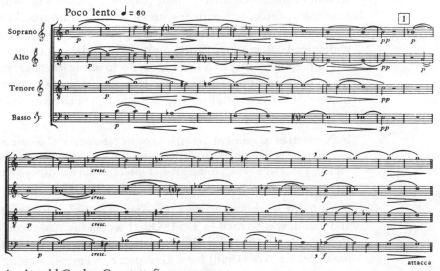

4 Arnold Cooke, *Quartett*, first movement

not always easy to handle, both because of their high pitch and because the relative lack of upper partials can produce combination and difference tones as well as flaws in intonation which are painfully obvious to the listener. Another factor which imposes restraints on the part-writing is that the soprano, alto, tenor and bass recorders differ by only a fourth or fifth in range and are very similar in timbre and tone-quality. Cooke handles this problem very well, creating a rich texture without shrillness and managing to give each instrument an independent and equally important line. Other compositions by Cooke which are worthy of note are the *Quartet* (1964) for alto recorder, violin, cello and piano, written for Carl Dolmetsch, and the *Serial Theme and Variations* (1966) for alto recorder solo. This is a perfect 'textbook' example of serialism according to the principles of Schoenberg and was written for Michael Vetter.

Hans Ulrich Staeps

The Austrian counterpart to Arnold Cooke is Hans Ulrich Staeps (1909–88), whose attitude to the recorder and whose prolific output for it is similar. Staeps was an active recorder player and teacher and this gave him a greater understanding of the instrument and its needs. His primary concern as a composer was to provide good music for the averagely-competent music-lover, leaving the provision of works for the professional player to others. It would be wrong, however, to underestimate the quality of his writing because of the modesty of his aims. Staeps's very large output of recorder music (more than twenty works over a period of thirty years) consists mainly of pieces for recorder consorts of three or four players, together with works for massed ensembles of recorders with or without other instruments. As well as this, his two books of technical exercises, *Das tägliche Pensum* and *Tonfiguren*, are in widespread use as a foundation for good recorder technique.

The preponderance of ensemble over solo music (there are only four works for solo recorder) reflects Staeps's strong belief in the importance of group music-making as a social activity, an attitude which he explained in an interview some years ago:

In the hands of qualified players the recorder can certainly become a significant concert instrument of considerable value, but . . . it is much more important to see it as a vehicle, a tool with which to help music-lovers obtain a conscious and active perception of melody and harmony in a relatively easy manner.   (Reichenthal 1980, 147)

Staeps' first work for recorder, the *Sonata in E flat major* for alto recorder and piano, was written in 1951. Other works for solo recorder include the *Virtuose Suite* (1961) for alto recorder solo and the *Sonata in C minor 'in modo preclassico'* (1968) for alto recorder and piano. Among several small-scale chamber works, the *Saratoga Suite* (1965) for soprano, alto and tenor recorders and the *Trio* (1972) for two alto and one tenor recorder deserve prominence. In a commentary on the *Saratoga Suite* (Staeps 1966, 5), the composer discusses his attempts to 'extract from the static tone of recorders those harmonic possibilities which had been discovered for the piano by the French Impressionists, Debussy and Ravel'. The harmonic ambiguity which he uses to create this effect is strongly marked in the *Saratoga Suite* and is backed up by clear rhythmic organisation which gives impetus to the music. The *Arkadische Szene* (1978) for recorder quintet shows a further progression in these ideas. *Aubade und Tanz* (1957) for SATB recorder sextet, guitar and piano was the first of a number of works for large recorder ensemble, a genre with which Staeps is particularly associated. The best known of these works are the *Chorisches Quintett* (1963) for recorder quintet doubled at the octave by a mixed quintet of woodwind and strings; the *Divertimento in D* (1957; rev. 1969) for four-part recorder choir, piano and percussion *ad lib*; the delightful *Des Einhorns Anmut* (1978) for twelve-part recorder ensemble and the *Berliner Sonate* (1979) for three-part octave-doubling recorder ensemble.

5 *The avant-garde*

Avant-garde recorder pieces began to appear in Germany and the Netherlands in the early 1960s, constituting, as they grew in numbers, a significant change in direction for the instrument. This does not mean that conventional styles were abandoned – such works continue to be written, and are very necessary and important for the survival of the recorder – but the first attempts of players and composers to investigate new playing techniques heralded the recognition of an area of unexplored potential and led to the subsequent development of the recorder as a twentieth-century rather than an historical instrument. This new attitude to instrumental technique was not unique to the recorder, but merely reflected an important facet of twentieth-century music at the time.

The important connotation in the adjectival use of the term avant-garde is the implication of rebellion against an established order and this was a clear motivation for many young composers in the 1960s. Another determining factor is the demands the work makes on the player. Avant-garde works tend to demand great versatility, involving playing (sometimes on several instruments), singing, speaking, dramatic effects, and so on, and although there are notable exceptions, such as the works of John Cage, the projection of the personality of the performer is often an important element. The label 'avant-garde' is sometimes used rather too loosely by recorder players to describe any work involving extended techniques; strictly speaking, it should be applied only to the innovative early pieces in this genre.

The first avant-garde recorder compositions were largely the result of the activities of the two leading players of the time, Michael Vetter and Frans Brüggen, and were written in the general atmosphere of experimentation which then prevailed among all instrumentalists. They were interested in contemporary music and wanted to branch out into other areas of performance beyond the confines of the renaissance and baroque repertoire. It was also very clear, to Brüggen in particular, that the early repertoire was not extensive enough nor interesting enough to be the basis for a serious solo career. Consequently, they began to commission works which could be included in their concerts. The composers Jürg Baur, Louis Andriessen and Rob du Bois were among the first to respond. Whereas previous compositions in conventional style had accepted the recorder at face value as a simple, lyrical melody instrument, these composers made a serious attempt to develop the full potential of the recorder as a sound source and were among the first to write for the instrument in a completely modern idiom, making no concessions to its supposed limitations. This was, of course, made possible by the fact that they were writing for players of very considerable technical accomplishment and sophisticated musical intelligence. Without this fortunate combination of players, composers, and opportunities for performance, the avant-garde recorder movement might not have gained momentum.

EARLIEST EXAMPLES

One of the earliest examples of an avant-garde recorder piece is *Muziek* (1961) for alto recorder solo by the Dutch composer Rob du Bois (b. 1934). Du Bois, an exact contemporary of Brüggen, for whom the work was written, trained as a pianist and is a self-taught composer. Performances of his music at contemporary music festivals in Zagreb, Warsaw and Prague in the late 1960s brought him some international acclaim and several works have been commissioned by the Dutch government. Du Bois uses twelve-note techniques and note-row procedures of various kinds; *Muziek* is based on successive transformations of a note row. Although the use of extended techniques is limited to flutter-tonguing, rustle tones, glissando and finger vibrato only (a relatively modest range of effects by comparison with later works by this and other composers), nevertheless a very high level of technical accomplishment is needed to execute the complex rhythms and awkward atonal patterns (Ex. 5). It is this uncompromising attitude to the limitations

5   Rob du Bois, *Muziek*

of the instrument which labels the piece as avant-garde. The full chromatic compass of the recorder is employed in a way that necessitates very great finger dexterity, since sharps and flats other than those occurring in the keys most closely related to the recorder's home key involve awkward forked and cross-fingerings which can be difficult at speed. Another feature is the very specific and detailed notation of articulation and dynamics. Passages such as that shown in Ex. 5 require a far greater precision and range of effects in tonguing than earlier works such as the Cooke *Concerto*, for instance, or the Badings *Sonata*, both written only a few years earlier. The level of dynamic control needed is also much greater. Du Bois calls for a range from *ppp* to *f* and although this cannot be taken completely literally, it is certainly possible to extend the dynamic range by using a recorder which can take changes of breath pressure without going out of tune and by employing non-standard fingerings.

At much the same time as du Bois was writing *Muziek* for Brüggen, Jürg Baur in Germany was composing the first of a number of recorder pieces for Vetter. This was *Incontri* (1960) for alto recorder and piano. Baur (b. 1918) achieved recognition rather late in life, his career having been interrupted by the Second World War. He adopted twelve-note techniques in the mid-1950s and is probably best known as the composer of the 'orchestral visions' *Quintetto Sereno* (1958) and *Romeo und Julia* (1962–3). In 1960 he was awarded a scholarship to study at the Villa Massimo in Rome. During this period he composed *Incontri* and another work for recorder, *Mutazioni*, as well as a piece for oboe and orchestra entitled *Concerto Romano*.

Incontri was written at the request of Michael Vetter and, while it does not use any extended techniques as such, the work does require a greater technical and interpretative range than was usual in German recorder music at the time. Baur's next work for recorder, *Mutazioni* (1962) was, however, a different matter. This is a serial work for solo alto recorder and consists of a theme and fourteen variations. Multiphonics,* glissandos and various forms of vibrato are used, as well as varied articulation, a wide dynamic range and the full chromatic compass of the instrument (Ex. 6). The form is indeterminate, the order of performing the variations being left to the player, and a number of the variations are improvisatory, requiring free interpretation of given note groups. This takes the recorder player into territory that was already familiar to players of other wind instruments through the compositions of Stockhausen, Nono, Berio and others, but was still entirely new for the hitherto conventional and stereotyped recorder.

A subsequent work by Baur, *Pezzi Uccelli* (1964) for solo recorder, is based

---

* *Multiphonic*. This term is used here, as in other studies of woodwind instruments, to denote a sound which is perceived by the ear as being composed of a complex group of differing pitches (see p. 89).

6   Jürg Baur, *Mutazioni*: © by Breitkopf & Härtel, Wiesbaden

on birdsong. This is the modern counterpart of a type of recorder music associated with birds for which there are many seventeenth- and eighteenth-century precedents. Examples such as the collection of tunes for singing birds, *The Bird Fancyer's Delight* (1717), and William Williams's *Sonata in imitation of birds* (1703), come to mind. Another modern instance is Hans-Martin Linde's *Music for a Bird* (see p. 60), in which extended techniques are used in a very evocative imitation of birdsong. *Pezzi Uccelli* dates from the time when Vetter was preparing his treatise on non-standard fingerings, *Il Flauto Dolce ed Acerbo* (Vetter 1969), and was obviously able to give the composer many ideas for the use of non-standard fingerings to play harmonics and multiphonics as well as to obtain variations in volume and timbre. Further innovatory techniques devised here, again presumably in consultation with Vetter, involve playing on recorders with the block displaced or with a piece of thin card inserted in the windway, effects which impede the airstream and distort the tone.

Sweet (1964) by Louis Andriessen (b. 1939) for alto recorder solo makes even greater demands on the player's technique. This influential work was composed for Brüggen and the title, with its punning reference to the baroque suite, mocks the traditional pastoral image of the recorder. This is not 'sweet music' and the main effect of the piece derives from the frenzied efforts of the performer to cope with the demands of the music. *Sweet* was deliberately conceived by Andriessen as an 'unplayable' piece, a sort of examination of the formidable qualities of virtuosity. It builds through some very rapid and difficult chromatic writing to a prolonged central climax, a 'black-out' where, in spite of frantic efforts, the soloist is unable to continue playing (Ex. 7). The mental state of the performer at this point is represented by an extended unspecified interruption, usually an auditory one in the form of continuous pre-recorded sound or noise effects, although visual and theatrical interruptions have also been used. When this has subsided the soloist resumes, trying but failing to re-establish the earlier impetus of the music.

Of all the works in the avant-garde repertoire, that which has become the most widely known is *Gesti* (1966) for alto recorder solo by Luciano Berio

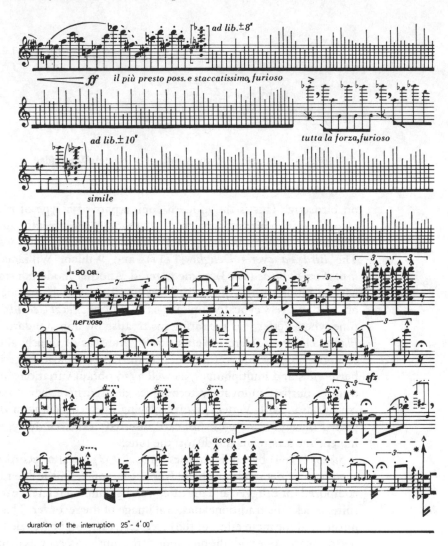

duration of the interruption 25″- 4′ 00″

✱ ↑ very high sound

7   Louis Andriessen, *Sweet*

(b. 1925). For many, *Gesti* ('Gestures') epitomises the revolution in recorder playing with its sudden and unpredictable shifts of register, vocal sounds, flutter-tonguing and spiky staccato notes. This is probably the most frequently performed of all avant-garde recorder works. Most professional players play it and Frans Brüggen, for whom it was written, has toured all over the world with it. By the time *Gesti* came to be written, the idea of playing contemporary music on the recorder was no longer quite so strange, at least to the performers, although it must be emphasised that audiences were still very unprepared for the new role of the recorder and the element of shock and sometimes antagonism was, therefore, all the greater. *Gesti* was very different from earlier avant-garde recorder compositions, not so much in its actual use of new techniques as in the whole concept of the work. The idea behind the composition is explained in a letter Berio wrote to Brüggen when sending him the original manuscript: 'I realise now that you are responsible for one of the strangest "gestures" of my life. As you can see I tried to celebrate a divorce between your fingers and your mouth . . .' (Brüggen 1966, 66). *Gesti* is, in fact, an exploration of what happens when the normally inseparable functions in wind-playing of breathing, tonguing and fingering are forced to act independently of one another so that the perfect co-ordination between faculties that the player has acquired through many years of training is deliberately destroyed. To set against this destructive element in the work is Berio's comment when Frans Brüggen first went to play for him to introduce him to the recorder: 'This is a very human instrument', he said, 'you don't get too angry, you don't get too happy or too loud . . .'. In a conversation with Brüggen in 1988 he added that he also had in mind a sort of *hommage* to all the strange guttural sounds in the Dutch language. One feels that *Gesti* was written as much for Brüggen with all his particular personal and musical attributes as for the recorder itself. However it was, Berio showed great insight into the intrinsic qualities of recorder sound, just as he did with his series of *Sequenzas* for various solo instruments, some of which were written during this period, also with specific performers in mind. *Gesti* is, in spirit, a member of this group.

With a duration of about six minutes, *Gesti* falls into three sections. It begins with only the faint tapping sounds of the fingers on the finger-holes. Then gradually, mouth activity is commenced and while the player fingers a rapid, repeated pattern, the mouth produces an unrelated and apparently random splatter of under- and over-blown notes, harmonics and multiphonics, mixed with vocal sounds. In the second section fingers and mouth begin to work together. The fingers are freed from their mechanical repetitive actions and increasingly in their movements come to parallel the pitch of the instrumental sounds. In the third section, the only one in conventional notation, fingering, tonguing and breathing are reunited and the work ends on a sung note, a final resolution of the struggle with the instrument, perhaps?

As is generally the case in works by Berio, the notation is precise, logical and individual. In *Gesti* each system of the score is divided into two horizontal bands assigned respectively to mouth and fingers. The upper band, denoting mouth activity, indicates three levels of breath pressure (low, medium and high) by means of the placing of note-heads in relation to two

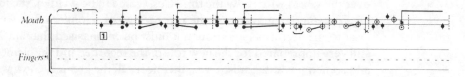

8 Luciano Berio, *Gesti*

parallel lines (Ex. 8). Note-heads can be black (instrumental sound), white (vocal sound) or a circle with black dot inside (simultaneous instrumental and vocal sound). Duration of notes is indicated by the length of the beams attached to them. Notes without beams denote short sounds, while notes with vertical strokes through the note-head are to be played 'as short as possible'. Time is shown in seconds on a horizontal line placed between the two bands of each system, except in the last section of the work which reverts to stave notation with a metronome marking. Dynamics are indicated on a scale of 1 to 7 with the numbers written on the score.

The second, lower band of each system shows finger activity. In the first section of the score this part is left blank because the finger activity consists entirely of the repetition of a rapid passage taken either from a baroque work (the *Giga* of Telemann's *Sonata in D minor* for recorder and basso continuo is suggested), or a pattern of the performer's own devising, provided that when combined with the mouth sounds, it gives a satisfactory range of harmonics. The repetition of a mechanical fingering pattern of this type, uncoordinated with breathing and tonguing, produces unpredictable results which vary from performance to performance. In the second section, fingering is indicated approximately by continuous lines running through three pitch bands, the outer limits of which are defined (Ex. 9).

From the performer's point of view *Gesti* is stimulating to prepare and difficult to play but it is questionable whether it is very memorable to audi-

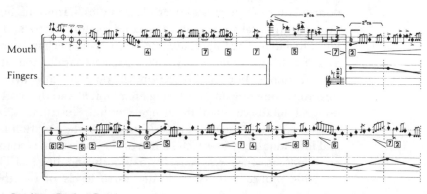

9 Luciano Berio, *Gesti*

ences other than as a display of technical virtuosity. There is a sense in which it is more a player's than a listener's piece. In early performances, lighting effects were used at the composer's suggestion in order to enhance the circus element in the work by isolating the player in a bright spotlight. Recently, with the growing acceptance of avant-garde music by audiences, performances of this and similar compositions tend to be assimilated into 'normal' recital programmes without comment of any kind, environmental or otherwise.

NEW TECHNIQUES

A particularly good example of the use of new instrumental techniques is provided by *Fragmente* (1968) for solo tenor recorder by the Japanese composer Makoto Shinohara (b. 1931). This work, which is written in open form, represents a further departure from the 'pre-avant-garde' norm because here the use of extended techniques is central to the whole concept of the work and their use is such as to produce ugly, aggressive and disturbing sounds as well as the gentler, expressive passages which are perhaps more often associated with the recorder. It also requires a considerable input on the part of the performer both in planning the sequence of musical material and in conveying the strong dramatic dimension which is such an important part of the work.

Shinohara studied composition with Messiaen and Stockhausen and has a particular interest in *musique concrète* and electronic music. He spent the year 1966 at Utrecht University working on electronic music and during this period came into contact with Frans Brüggen, to whom *Fragmente* is dedicated. It may be supposed that Brüggen and Shinohara had some discussion about the piece during the course of its composition and Brüggen must have suggested and demonstrated playing techniques to Shinohara as well as perhaps influencing him in his choice of tenor rather than alto recorder. There are few modern works for solo tenor, but this particular instrument is well suited to the avant-garde with its deep 'woody' timbre, and it and the bass recorder are now being used more and more frequently.

The title ('fragments') refers to the construction of the work, which consists of fourteen short units or fragments of musical material which may be linked in a sequence of the performer's own choosing, subject to certain restrictions laid down by the composer. For instance, certain fragments may not be played at the beginning or end of the performance while others, such as fragment 10, which contains very high overblown sounds and a sustained and dramatic passage of random finger-play, may only be played after the mid-point of the performance. Each fragment is played once only and, unless otherwise indicated, all fragments are linked without a break. A complete performance of all the fragments takes eight to nine minutes but a shorter version, which should consist of at least eight fragments, is permissible. The work, however, is indeterminate only in form. All other elements – pitch, note-durations, technical execution and musical interpretation – are notated precisely. Open forms of this type, where the musical material is specified but the arrangement of it is left to the performer, were first seen in the 1950s in such works as Earle Brown's *25 Pages* (1953) and Stockhausen's *Klavierstück XI* (1956). In these works the circumstances and impulses of performance largely dictate the ordering of the musical material and the element of chance is therefore considerable. The performance sequence of *Fragmente*, on the other hand, is intended to be prepared in advance, and the limitations imposed by Shinohara on the use of musical material mean that although every interpretation is different, certain structural and musical elements always dominate the performance.

Fragmente is constructed so that each unit demonstrates a different technique and a different type of sound, e.g. multiphonics, overblown sounds, microtones, flutter-tonguing, glissando, random finger-play, finger slaps and so on (Ex. 10). The construction of the fragments is carefully thought out so that they will dovetail satisfactorily in a variety of ways, and the pauses placed at the end of fragments 1, 3, 7, 8, 10, and 14 ensure that the work falls into a number of subsections no matter what the chosen sequence. The melodic material utilises a number of related motifs constructed from fourths, sevenths and their inversions and this gives coherence to the work. The work is basically in conventional staff notation with note-durations indicated proportionally, while time is indicated either by giving the duration of a fragment or portion of a fragment in seconds or by the use of conventional

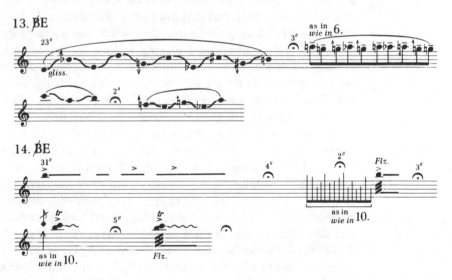

10   Makoto Shinohara, *Fragmente*

note-values with a metronome marking. Where necessary, comments on technical and interpretative aspects of the work accompany each fragment. Interestingly, the use of vibrato in the performance of the work is specifically forbidden in the composer's introduction. This directive would probably not be thought necessary nowadays, but in the mid- to late-1960s vibrato was still considered to be a part of normal recorder tone-production, giving a rather romantic, flute-like quality which is now felt to be against the nature of the instrument.

A later example of a similar compositional concept applied to a consort piece is seen in *Arrangements* (1975–6) by the Polish composer Kazimierz Serocki (1922–81). *Arrangements* consists of seventeen separate segments, each occupying one page of score, which may be played in any order. The number of participants is also variable and a different selection of segments is made according to whether there are one, two, three or four performers. A multiple performance is also possible, with different instrumental groupings playing their versions simultaneously in interconnected rooms, and the audience free to move between them. The work is highly dependent on extended techniques: all are notated with characteristic precision by Serocki, some being represented by symbols which are unique to him. It is a complex but very carefully-thought-out framework for a composition that, by its very nature, will always present a different end-result at each performance

OTHER SIGNIFICANT COMPOSITIONS

Apart from the works already discussed, which are landmarks in modern recorder music, a great many other new compositions made their appearance during the 1960s, continuing and consolidating the development of new styles and techniques in recorder playing. After *Muziek*, Rob du Bois composed several further recorder pieces which are worthy of mention. *Spiel und Zwischenspiel* (1962) was written for Michael Vetter and is a difficult work for recorder and piano involving harmonics, multiphonics, white noise, glissandos and various forms of vibrato including throat vibrato, all techniques which were developed in collaboration with Vetter. *Pastorale II* (1963–9) for recorder, flute and guitar and *Pastorale VII* (1964) for alto recorder solo followed. These belonged to a set of pastorales for various instrumental combinations written in the 1960s, and are interesting in that they show the composer coming to terms with the novelty of his material and reaching a much greater refinement and economy in his use of recorder techniques as well as in musical content.

Louis Andriessen's graphic composition for flute and piano, *Paintings* (1965), was adopted by Michael Vetter for performance on recorder and piano; this was approved by the composer because he felt that the recorder had far more potential for the production of new and exciting sounds than the flute. Will Eisma (b. 1929), another Dutchman, wrote a series of interesting works, all of which stretched the recorder technically. The first of these, *Affairs II* (1963), is for recorders (one player) and double-manual harpsichord (rather than piano) and is dedicated to Brüggen. This work falls into two sections entitled 'Report' and 'Phrases'. 'Report' is in conventional notation but 'Phrases' uses proportional notation and incorporates improvisatory sections. Eisma's next work for recorder, *Wonderen zijn schaars* (1965), for recorder and piano, developed the improvisatory element still further. The title, 'Miracles are rare', refers to the difficulties of the recorder part which the composer feels can only be overcome with miraculous assistance. The main difficulty encountered attaches to an improvised cadenza for recorder and piano which is notated graphically and in which the recorder player can bring in other wind instruments such as pitch pipe, swannee whistle, whistle, etc. while the pianist adds various devices such as brushes, metal foil, weights, corks, etc. to the strings of the piano (Ex. 11).

One of the important figures in the development of modern recorder music in Europe is Hans-Martin Linde. Among his many compositions for recorder are two works which are widely known and played. *Music for a Bird* (1968) for alto recorder solo is a very beautiful evocation of birdsong, consisting of seven short movements which use multiphonics, glissandos, trills, tremolos and all sorts of tricks with vibrato, articulation and vocal sounds (Ex. 12). *Amarilli mia bella* (1971) for one recorder soloist playing soprano, alto and bass recorders is a more elaborate and extended work. Subtitled 'Hommage à Johann Jacob van Eyck', it is based on a set of variations by this Dutch seventeenth-century carillon and recorder player. In 1646 van Eyck published *Der Fluyten Lusthof* ('The Flute's Pleasure Garden'), a collection of variations on well-known tunes, including the song 'Amarilli mia bella' by

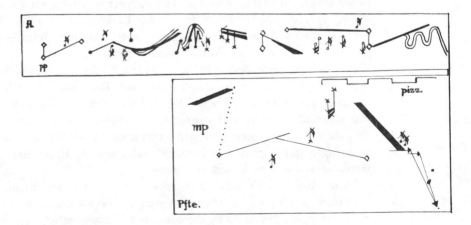

11   Will Eisma, *Wonderen zijn schaars*

12   Hans-Martin Linde, *Music for a Bird*, no. 1

Caccini, on which Linde based his composition. The piece is not so much 'variations on variations' as a re-interpretation of the van Eyck in the musical vocabulary of today. It uses all the extended techniques found in *Music for a Bird* together with some others such as random finger-play, microtones, and percussive effects. The idea of changing recorders during the course of a work was not then such a common occurrence as it is nowadays and playing successively on alto, soprano and bass recorders enlarged both the range and the timbres available to the composer.

Another figure who has been prolific in his use of new ideas is the German player-composer, Gerhard Braun (b. 1932), who since the late 1960s has been one of the main exponents of extended techniques, in many ways taking on the mantle of Michael Vetter, who was by then moving on to other interests. Braun studied at the Staatliche Hochschule für Musik in Stuttgart and later studied composition in Darmstadt with Konrad Lechner, who has himself written a number of recorder works. In addition to flute and recorder teaching at the Musikhochschule in Karlsruhe and editorial work for the music publisher Moeck, Braun has written a short book about modern recorder music (Braun 1978) as well as articles on various historical and contemporary topics.

Among the twenty or so works Braun has written for recorders, three stand out from the rest: *Monologe I* (1968–70) for one recorder player, *Nachtstücke* (1972) for recorder player and pianist, and *Schattenbilder* (1980) for alto recorder solo. *Monologe I*, Braun's first work for the instrument, is scored for alto recorder but may be played on any other member of the family or on several recorders successively. This gives the performer an important degree of freedom in choosing the actual instrumentation of the piece. The performer is also involved to a certain extent in the compositional process by being given a choice as to what material is included and in what sequence. The work consists of three main sections (A, B and C) which are in turn made up of a series of small fragments of musical material which can be linked in various ways according to guidelines suggested by the composer. Altogether, the piece represents a progression from ordered, specific musical sounds in section A through a mixture of pitched and unpitched sounds in B to noise in C. In this final section a prepared tape of recorder sounds may be used containing either unused material from the first section or material which has already been used but with rhythmic alterations. Braun has devised a number of new techniques which he uses here, particularly in the second and third sections, which involve playing on parts of the dismantled recorder. Among these are pitched sounds and noise produced by blowing into the head-piece as well as blowing 'à la cornetto' into the tube of the instrument (head-joint removed) as into a trumpet mouthpiece. Words are also spoken and whispered into the tube.

Nachtstücke departs somewhat from the abstractions of Braun's earlier works. As the name ('Night pieces') suggests, the music contains a number of nocturnal associations – an owl hooting, a nightingale's song, a clock striking, and many strange and unidentifiable night noises, including various rustling and rattling sounds which may be thought of as representing the cries and movements of animals. How far the performers wish to take these ideas is entirely up to them, but there is considerable potential for dramatic input. The piece consists of five short movements of approximately equal length, each of which is played on one of the five main members of the recorder family – sopranino, soprano, alto, tenor and bass. For the recorder player the technique is reasonably straightforward but the piano is prepared in various ways and the pianist plays on the strings inside the piano as well as on the keyboard.

Schattenbilder ('Silhouettes'), subtitled 'Five Meditations', deals with the idea of 'the end of all' (*rien ne va plus*), the disintegration of music into noise and finally silence. The piece makes much use of extended recorder techniques such as vibrato, flutter-tonguing, harmonics, mouth-sounds, percussive effects, etc. The piece demands some versatility, since the player also needs several small percussion instruments.

By the end of the 1960s, recorder playing was a very different affair to what it had been at the beginning of the decade. Frans Brüggen had achieved worldwide recognition as a recorder virtuoso and his playing and teaching had attracted many followers. Michael Vetter had, through his performance of works like *Spiral* with the Stockhausen-Ensemble, taken the recorder into the vanguard of contemporary music. David Munrow and The Early Music Consort of London had attracted a following for the recorder through their exuberant performances of early consort music. Standards of playing and teaching began to rise as a younger generation of players emerged, of whom Walter van Hauwe, Kees Boeke and Michala Petri are among the best-known. So much new composition had the effect of opening up the recorder repertoire to new ideas. Players were spurred on to develop their technique in order to cope with the demands of the new music and to show that the recorder was more than just a vehicle for restrained baroque music. Dissemination of information about new recorder techniques was slow at first and there was much duplication of effort to be seen in the avant-garde works of the 1960s, with effects being 'discovered' several times over. By the early 1970s, however, there can have been few players who were unaware of the revolution in recorder playing and as extended techniques became more familiar so their use became less haphazard and more considered.

This is noticeable in the recorder music of the mid to late 1970s, where extended techniques were, in most cases, used more sparingly and more effectively than in the music of the 1960s. Indeed it is part of the trend of contemporary music in general, where the sometimes excessive experimentation of the 1960s and early 1970s gave way to a more reasoned use of new techniques and ideas towards the end of the latter decade. Gerhard Braun's compositions, for instance, illustrate this development. His early works such as *Monologe I* and *Minimal Music II* (1971–2) present so many new ideas simultaneously that coherence tends to be obscured, but later works such as *Schattenbilder*, while still employing a wide range of extended techniques, do so with more restraint and for a clearly defined purpose. Other composers have made similar progressions in their musical thinking. For instance, Jacques Bank's many very novel pieces of the 1960s and early 1970s (see p. 70) were succeeded by compositions in which new techniques appear only very occasionally, if at all. Examples are *Two* (1979) for bass recorder and piano; *Maraens Trompetten* (1980) for two recorders and tape; and *Recorders* (1981) for solo recorder, strings and percussion. This does not mean that avant-garde recorder techniques were being rejected by composers, but rather that they were being used with more discretion. It is also clear that the 1970s saw a growing preoccupation with other aspects of music such as the dramatic possibilities of musical performance and the opportunities presented by electronics; as we shall see, it is in these areas that the main developments in recorder music in the 1970s occurred.

6 *The theatrical element*

The expansion in instrumental techniques which took place in the 1960s was accompanied by a growing concern on the part of composers for the visual and dramatic aspects of musical performance. Music theatre, as it was quickly labelled, required performers who were not just musicians but who could act, sing, dance, mime, etc. and who took part in theatrical/musical 'happenings' which could also include lighting effects, film and slide projections and the use of props and costumes. The actions of the performers and the reactions (and sometimes participation) of the audience became, in these performances, an integral part of the total experience. John Cage and Mauricio Kagel led the way in this new movement with such works as Cage's *Theatre Piece* (1960) for a variable group of performers and Kagel's *Sur Scène* (1959–60) for speaker, mime, recorded tape, singer and three instrumentalists. Other composers who wrote theatre pieces at about the same time were Berio (*Circles*, 1960) and Stockhausen (*Originale*, 1961).

Although there are few works in the modern recorder repertoire which can be labelled as music theatre pieces in the strict sense of the term, the influence of the music theatre ethos is clearly to be seen in an increased emphasis on the visual and dramatic dimension of many recorder works of the mid to late 1960s and afterwards, taking the form of a much greater use of speech, singing and movement in compositions which are, officially, instrumental works. One of the few examples of a true music theatre piece using recorder is *RARA*, the fruit of a collaboration between Sylvano Bussotti and Michael Vetter. This remarkable work, which is discussed in detail on p. 73, is written for a recorder player and a mime artist and has a very unusual graphic score. At the time it was written it represented a major departure for the recorder in that it took the instrument into the forefront of one of the most up-to-date areas of contemporary music.

Details IV (1975) by Franz Furrer-Münch (b. 1924) for recorder, cello or gamba, and organ is another, but less exotic example of music theatre. The composer's aim here is to combine action, gesture, speech, etc. in an integrated way with instrumental sounds. While it is possible to perform the work as a purely instrumental piece or with the addition of amplification and live electronics but without theatre effects, the composer feels that a purely instrumental performance is 'introverted', whereas a performance with theatre effects is 'extroverted' and is altogether to be preferred. In the latter mode of performance the players must 'make direct use of all the communicative events, together with their contradictory interpretations, that arise from the beginning of rehearsal'. Thus 'a catalogue of experienced or conjectural events and expressions is built up' from anything that may happen in the rehearsal period (Furrer-Münch: *Details IV*, Introduction). Every kind of 'music action' can be included – noise or notes – as well as 'mishaps' such as broken strings, sticking organ keys, dropped objects, etc. which may have happened accidentally at first but can then be incorporated into the performance. In addition, movement, speech, gestures, etc. such as getting up and going over to another player, or making signals of various kinds may also be employed. All these actions can be heightened and varied 'even to the point of absurdity' and a close personal interaction with events and actions of other players is important in ensuring that the performance becomes more than just the mechanical reproduction of a score. The composer also mentions the possibility of incorporating words built up by repetition, substitution and rearrangement into a 'universally valid statement, whose interpretation is left to each listener personally . . . '.

The work falls into six short continuous sections, the order of which may be changed according to the performers' preferences. Alternatively, a single section may be played on its own as 'minimal art'. The sections are contrasting in mood and content and the duration of the work is free, although the suggested minimum duration is approximately four minutes. If the order of the movements given in the score is preserved, the overall structure is that of an arch. The score consists of a mixture of graphic and indicative (symbol) notation. Graphic notation is used to show sound-effects for which the method of production is more-or-less self-evident, for example, note clusters, glissandos, multiphonics, etc., while symbols are used to indicate specific actions such as bowing beyond the bridge, pizzicato, etc. (Ex. 13). The recorder part may be played on any or all of the instruments of the recorder family and the techniques used include glissandos and multi-sound glissandos, multiphonics, very high sounds and harmonics. Cello and organ also employ extended techniques. For cello these include bowing on and beyond the bridge, bowing 'col legno', harmonics, scordatura and resonating pizzicato. Organ techniques include noise effects, 'TV whistle', sound oscillation, rumbling sounds and a 'Mass bell' effect. For performances where an organ is not available, an electronic keyboard with a good organ stop is an adequate substitute. It is worth noting that the instruments used in *Details IV* are those of the typical baroque conformation of solo instrument with basso continuo. Even though the treatment is rather different in this case, the instru-

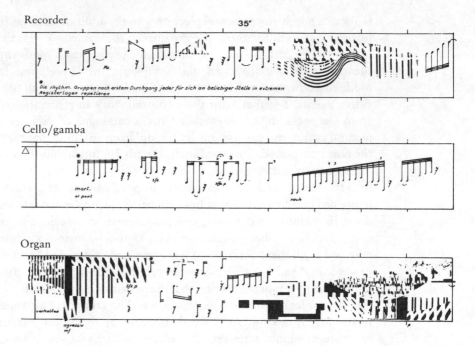

13   Franz Furrer-Münch, *Details IV*

ments combine well together, showing that the possibilities of this grouping are by no means exhausted.

FOCUS ON THE PERFORMER

In *Details IV* the theatrical element is explicit and central to the whole work. In other recorder pieces, however, it is less overt. In some cases it consists solely of the use of successive members of the recorder family in the course of a work, with the player changing instruments in a deliberate and dramatic manner. *Katalog* (1965) for one recorder player by Werner Heider (b. 1930) is an early example of this. Here the change of instruments is accomplished in such a way as to invest with significance the action of putting down one recorder and taking up another, thus reinforcing the aural effect of the change of register and timbre with a visual impression. A more important influence of music theatre has been the tendency to have a soloist play other instruments as well as the recorder in the course of the performance either consecutively or, in some cases, simultaneously. There are several examples of this. In *Comme l'on s'amuse bien* (1978) by Herman Rechberger (b. 1947), for instance, the soloist plays recorder, bells, wind chimes and mouth organ, speaks and sings, and also controls four metronomes. A similar situation

66

arises in *Notturno* (1977) by Martin Gümbel (1923–86), where the soloist plays bass recorder and also sings and plays two gongs. This work requires a play-back of taped material and, unless an assistant is available, the performer must control the tape recorder too.

One effect of works such as *Notturno*, *Katalog* and others has been to divert attention away from an exclusive concentration on the recorder and to focus it more on the player as a personality. Many works of the late 1960s and the early 1970s carry the specific designation 'for one recorder player' as opposed to the more usual forms such as 'for alto recorder' or 'for tenor recorder and piano', etc. and this is indicative of a change of attitude on the part of composers. The danger here is that a preoccupation with theatre and special effects can diminish the musical content and reduce the performance to a succession of circus tricks. Only the best composers have succeeded in avoiding this risk.

A prime example of the latter is *Black Intention* (1975) by the Japanese composer, Maki Ishii (b. 1936). This is one of the most convincing solo pieces in the repertoire structurally, technically and dramatically and has been very successful with both performers and audiences. The musical content and the whole concept of the work place it among the handful of truly great contemporary recorder compositions. Ishii studied composition in Japan and later in Berlin with Blacher and Rufer. He has also worked in electronic music in Japan and is active as an organiser of concerts of new music both in Japan and in Europe. His compositional style is characterised by a fusion of Japanese and Western ideas and influences and he is particularly skilful in the use of instrumental colour. He has written several works in which Japanese instruments such as shakuhachi, biwa, etc. are used with Western instruments, for example *Nucleus* (1973).

There is an interesting philosophical concept behind *Black Intention*. Ishii's idea was to portray people's reactions to the upsets and problems of daily life. Thus, the first part of the work represents the average person's reaction to adversity, where the unequal struggle produces negative consequences, while in the second part he portrays how the Buddhist approaches similar events, taming and thus conquering himself.

To represent this complex idea Ishii employs an unusual instrumentation for the solo performer: two soprano recorders played simultaneously, tenor recorder, tam-tam and voice. The first part is based on a simple village-style Japanese folk tune, played on a modern-pitch soprano recorder. This cheerful tune is abruptly disturbed by the entrance of the second soprano recorder, held in the player's other hand but playing at a pitch a semitone lower. Beginning with sustained notes and then progressing to a parallel duplication of the melody line, its increasingly alienating effect builds up inexorably until it results in complete 'burn-out' at a shatteringly loud and high-pitched climax, culminating in a stroke on the gong (Ex. 14). After a long pause, during which

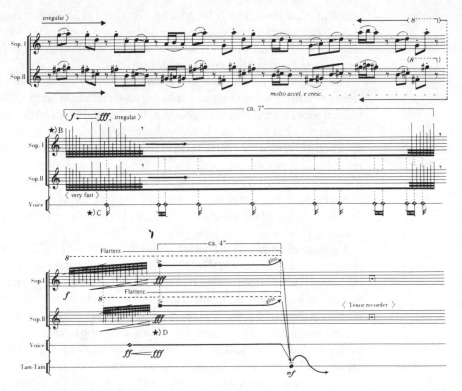

14   Maki Ishii, *Black Intention*

the sound of the gong gradually fades, the player commences part two, playing a tenor recorder in a very quiet and dream-like sequence of sustained low
notes accompanied by simultaneous soft sung notes 'like sighing' which are
coloured by three different speeds or types of vibrato. Into the meditative
section the folk-tune gradually breaks, first in fragments and then reasserting
itself in its entirety to complete the work (Ex. 15).

The mechanics of coping with the instrumentation are a problem which the
performer must solve with due regard to the visual and dramatic aspects of his
or her actions. In the first part, the compass of the folk melody is restricted (it
uses only the notes *g''*, *a''*, *c'''* and *d'''*, together with *b''* which appears as
an ornamental rather than as a melody note, and their octave transpositions)
and because of this the entire melody can be played using the fingers and
thumb of one hand only. This makes it possible for the performer to take up
the second, baroque-pitch recorder, placing it in the mouth together with the
first recorder and fingering it with the free hand. As the central climax begins
to build up, the player's voice is also used in various improvisatory guttural
sounds, culminating in a long *ff–fff* voice-sound which has been interpreted
by some players, notably Walter van Hauwe, as a terrifying roar in the style

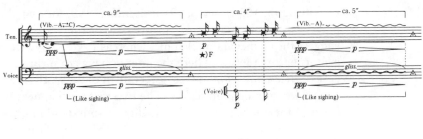

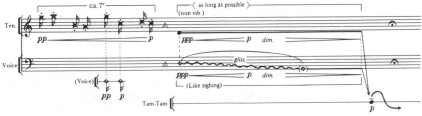

15   Maki Ishii, *Black Intention*

of the Japanese Noh-theatre. The resounding stroke on the gong which immediately follows this is perhaps the most tricky moment of the perform- ance. The player is holding two soprano recorders and must rapidly and neatly transfer them to one hand or put them down and equally rapidly pick up a beater with which to hit the gong, all without interrupting the musical and dramatic flow. The gong is usually placed behind or to one side of the player with the beater and tenor and soprano recorders on a small table nearby. All this should be accomplished in a suitably stylised manner. Some performers have wished to accentuate this with various props and costumes and with lighting effects and it is certainly advisable to give consideration to the visual dimension for the sake of the audience. Walter van Hauwe has even used theatrical smoke to be released at the moment of the central climax.

Black Intention is strongly influenced by Japanese traditional music, not just in the melodic material but also in the sounds, atmosphere and theatrical dimension of the performance. Certain elements are particularly character- istic: for instance, the use of long, sustained sounds with very subtle timbre changes and microtonal colouring, derived from the music of the shakuhachi, and the high overblown sounds which are typical of the Noh-flute. The gradual accelerandos which Ishii employs are also very characteristic of Japanese music, as are the glissandos and the various speeds and intensities of vibrato. The tam-tam or large gong is, of course, an oriental instrument.

This technique of playing on two recorders at once has been used occasion- ally, and generally with success, by other composers as well as Ishii. Some examples are *Recorder Music* (1973) for recorder and tape by Peter

69

Dickinson (b. 1934) (see p. 79) and *Ende* (1980) for two alto recorders (one player) by Louis Andriessen. In the case of the Dickinson the idea was to suggest the medieval double pipe, whereas *Ende* was written for Brüggen as a short encore piece and here the intention was to surprise and amuse. In the case of *Black Intention* the musical content of the work is such as to reject any suggestion of mere gimmickry. The two recorders appear to have been used because they gave a particular quality of sound, adding the right degree of distortion and alienation to the music by the clash of tuning without altering the timbre in any major way. All in all, this composition is a striking example of an original concept where strong and convincing ideas are worked out very successfully.

VOCAL/INSTRUMENTAL TECHNIQUES

The Dutch composer Jacques Bank (b. 1943) assigns a similarly dramatic role to the recorder player. The area in which Bank has been particularly innovative is that of simultaneous singing and playing on the recorder, that is, using the player's breath to produce a vocal as well as an instrumental sound. Bank's preoccupation with the availability of these two quite distinct sound sources, the instrument and the voice, contained within one performer has been developed in many of his works for recorder and has inevitably involved the use of texts also, unorthodox as this is in instrumental music. Apart from Michael Vetter, who has used similar vocal/instrumental techniques in *Rezitative*, few other composers have made use of this particular device.

Bank has, so far, written ten works using recorder, generally in combination with other instruments rather than as a solo instrument. This argues an unusually consistent interest in the instrument over the twenty years or so of his career to date. More than half of these works are dedicated to the Dutch recorder player and teacher Baldrick Deerenberg (b. 1946), a former student of Frans Brüggen and a friend and contemporary of Bank, and this connection with a player who was able and willing to perform his works was clearly an important stimulus. Bank studied composition with Ton de Leeuw and Jos Kunst, gaining the composition prize of the Amsterdam Conservatory in 1974 and, although not widely known as a composer cither in the Netherlands or abroad, his output, apart from the recorder pieces, includes works for piano, organ, orchestra, chorus with orchestra, and various combinations of chamber instruments. In his compositions he uses note-rows and serial procedures influenced, no doubt, by his studies with de Leeuw.

One of his early works, *The Memoirs of a Cyclist* (1967, revised 1970) for two recorder players, is perhaps best described as a sort of dramatic sketch with music. Inspired by a newspaper account of the life and exploits of the

The theatrical element

Irish professional cyclist Séamus Elliott, *The Memoirs of a Cyclist* strives to portray the anguish of a man for whom fame and fortune have changed to isolation and disgrace. Elliott reached the height of his fame as a racing cyclist in the years 1960–4, attaining folk-hero status. His career was abruptly terminated, however, when the discovery that he was taking stimulants to help him win races coincided with his arrest by Interpol for drug-smuggling. Overnight Elliott's reputation was destroyed and he returned to Ireland to live in seclusion. A portion of his memoirs was later serialised in a popular English weekly paper and from this Bank has taken the following lines, which are used as a text in this work: 'I am a fugitive in the green hills of Ireland. I don't go out. I don't answer the phone and I lie to people that I'm on holiday! Some holiday! When I look at those narrow Wicklow lanes I see instead the long, hot, dusty roads of France. On those I made my name and crashed to disaster.' The dramatic possibilities of this subject matter are obviously considerable and in addition, as the composer remarks in his introduction to the score, the satirical nature of the work should receive due attention.

The piece, which is short, is based on a six-note row producing much disjunct movement and with widely-varying and exaggerated dynamic contrasts. It consists of three sections and a spoken introduction and the two performers, both playing alto recorders, use a mixture of speech and *Sprechgesang* to convey Elliott's words in English together with a commentary on them in Dutch. In certain places spoken or chanted words are interspersed with instrumental notes so that the players are constantly switching, without a break, from singing to playing and back again. The piece also contains its share of extended recorder techniques: flutter-tonguing, glissandos, random finger-play, overblown sounds, and notes played with the end-hole stopped.

Bank's interest in cycling also inspired *Put me on my bike no. 1* (1971) for solo baritone, alto recorder and SATB choir (sixteen voices). This time the subject is the English rider Tom Simpson, whose last words, before he died at the top of a mountain pass in France during a race, are said to have been 'Put me on my bike'. This piece is essentially for *a cappella* chorus with solo voice and recorder obbligato, again based on a note-row. As well as normal vocal sounds, the singers are required to use a range of other techniques such as clapping, foot-stamping, whistling, whispering, speaking and tapping the hand over the mouth while singing to produce a tremolo effect. Special techniques employed in the recorder part include quarter tones, overblown sounds (monophonic and multiphonic), notes played with stopped and open end-hole, vibrato, and breathy flutter-tonguing. In measures 215–65 the recorder player is asked to sing and play (simultaneously) two distinct melodic lines, notated graphically on two separate staves (Ex. 16). Amplification is also required, both to balance the sound and to make possible the extremes of dynamics necessary throughout the work.

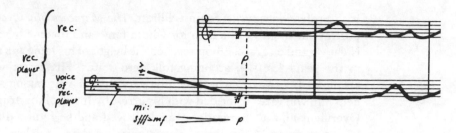

16   Jacques Bank, *Put me on my bike no. 1*

GRAPHIC SCORES

The use of graphics in the notation of twentieth-century music has been a very significant development in that it allows performers freedom of interpretation while at the same time encouraging them to use creative ideas of their own. As a result, the musical barriers between composer and performer have been lowered, with composers relinquishing some of their authority over the final shape of works and performers accepting greater responsibility in the shaping of the performance. Works such as Morton Feldman's *Projections* (1950–1), Earle Brown's *December 1952* and *Folio* (1952–3), and John Cage's *Water Music* (1952) were among the first and most innovatory graphic compositions. Later, other composers adopted this method too. Examples are Haubenstock-Ramati's *Mobile for Shakespeare* (1959), Logothetis's *Agglomeration* (1960), and Renosto's *Players* (1967).

In the recorder repertoire many composers mix graphic and non-graphic elements in their works, for example *Details IV* by Franz Furrer-Münch, and *Comme l'on s'amuse bien* and *Dolce ma non troppo!* (1979–80) by Herman Rechberger. Few composers of recorder music have expressed their ideas entirely in graphics and there is only a handful of works of this type in the repertoire, mainly from the 1960s. Nevertheless they form a significant group because of their influence in breaking down the stereotyped image of the recorder.

Michael Vetter is the player most associated with the performance of graphic works for recorder. Some of his own compositions are graphic, for example, *Figurationen III* and *Rezitative*. He was also responsible for the preparation for publication of the recorder version of Louis Andriessen's *Paintings* and was involved as collaborator in the composition of *RARA* by Sylvano Bussotti. For Vetter in the 1960s, graphics united his two main interests of painting and music, and his investigations into non-standard recorder fingerings and their application in the production of new sounds meant that he was both eager to find works in which to display his technique and improvisatory skills and uniquely qualified to play them.

His first experience of improvisation from a graphic score arose from his meeting in Florence in 1964 with the Italian avant-garde composer Sylvano Bussotti (b. 1931). At that time Bussotti was beginning work on his music-theatre piece *La Passion selon Sade*, and their meeting led to the inclusion in this work of an interlude for recorder and mime. This was entitled *RARA* (1966) and, according to Vetter, was conceived as a collaboration between Bussotti and himself in which Bussotti prepared the graphics and Vetter translated them into conventional notation, basing his interpretation on the ideas they had discussed at their original meeting.

La Passion selon Sade (1965–6) is a music drama somewhere on the borders between opera and chamber music. It is written for a small group of performers, all of whom have multiple functions as musicians, actors, singers, mime-artists, etc. and embodies a radical conception of theatre which was very new in the mid 1960s. It is based on a sixteenth-century French sonnet and the principal soloist, a mezzo-soprano, represents both of de Sade's female characters, Justine and Juliette. This dark and decadent work is typical of Bussotti's bizarre style of composition and of his increasing use of erotic themes and texts during the 1960s. Each page of the *Passion* is an elaborate piece of art-work in Bussotti's own very distinctive graphic style which mixes lettering, symbols and drawings with some very unconventional uses of traditional notation. *RARA* occupies a single, very carefully-prepared page of this score and forms an interlude in the main action of the drama. It is intended to be performed by a recorder player and a mime artist, although it can also be played as a solo concert piece for recorder alone. In the latter case, as Michael Vetter remarks in his introduction to the separately-published Ricordi edition of *RARA*, it should be regarded as a 'quintessential distillation' of the ideas of the *Passion*.

The *RARA* page, one of the most strikingly unusual scores in the whole modern recorder repertoire, presents in one integrated pictorial concept all the information necessary for performance and is, in fact, much more specific in its notation than might at first appear (Ex. 17). Unlike other sections of the *Passion* no staff notation is used. Instead, the score is composed of the letters 'R' and 'A' in random combinations as well as forming the word 'rara', together with arrows and lozenges. These components are arranged in boxes and the score can be played in any or all of the four possible orientations of the page. By using four different types of lettering (solid, outline, dashed and dotted) as well as upper and lower case characters, sixteen different types of sound can be notated from the letters R and A. These include harmonics, rustle tones, normal sounds with harsh and soft timbres, and single sounds as well as multiphonics. Arrows and lozenges are used to indicate glissandos and 'extra effects' respectively. In fact, the quality of sound is notated more specifically than the other elements of the music such as pitch and note-duration. These latter parameters are to be taken as proportional to the written dimensions of the letters and symbols.

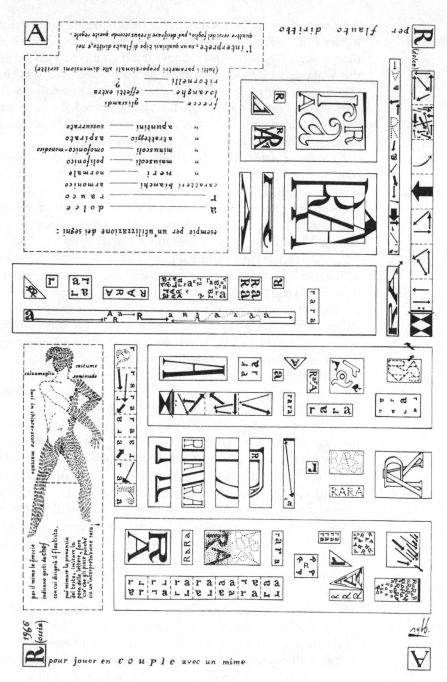

17   Sylvano Bussotti, *RARA*

As well as their function as symbols for particular types of sound material, the use of the letters R and A and the word 'rara' carried further connotations. The suggestion of 'strangeness' and of 'alienation' is implied in the similarity to the Italian words *raro* (exceptional, rare, uncommon) and *rarità* (curiosity, rarity) developed from the same root. In the directions to the mime included in the score Bussotti says 'può mimare la pronunzia del testo, imitare la posa delle lettere, fare ciò gli piace purchè sia un'interpretazione rara' ('He can mime the pronunciation of the text, the shape or attitude of the letters, do whatever he likes because it is a strange interpretation'). Furthermore, these letters are the initials of Bussotti's friend Romano Amidei and the 'rara' motif derived from them occurs in a number of Bussotti's other works.

The realisation for performance of a work such as this is complicated in the extreme. *RARA* was not intended to be a spur-of-the-moment improvisation; it needs to be carefully worked out and written down. There is considerable scope for the inventive use of all the new techniques and the success or failure of a performance rests largely on the ability of the player to make a convincing interpretation. In a performance with mime the coordination of these roles must be planned with care, but the dramatic impact of the work is undoubtedly heightened by the addition of a visual dimension. In order to arrive at his realisation, Vetter has given a numbered sequence to the boxes of material in the score and has assigned pitches, note-durations and types of sound in accordance with the composer's instructions. Vetter claims that this version of *RARA* is a full collaboration with Bussotti. In the introductory notes to the score he says '[this] is not an improvisation, it is an exact translation of Bussotti's drawing, and is therefore a joint composition in the full sense of the word'. Vetter's insistence on the authenticity of his version above all others is something of a contradiction in view of the fact that graphic scores, by their very nature, are indeterminate and therefore have no 'right' or 'wrong' interpretation, merely a succession of events. Furthermore, if all recorder players are to play only Vetter's realisation, the *raison d'être* of Bussotti's score is entirely removed. Significantly, in the full score of the *Passion* only the graphics are given and no reference is made to the existence of a written-out realisation.

In Vetter's own graphic composition *Rezitative* (1967) problems of interpretation also arise, in this case with the added complications of a contact microphone attached to the recorder and live electronic manipulation of the sound. Written the year after Vetter had received the score of *RARA* from Bussotti, *Rezitative* shows several similarities, particularly in the use of different fields of material arranged to form an overall graphic pattern and in the use of letters of various shapes and sizes to form words and fragments of words (Ex. 18). The visual impact of *Rezitative* is very striking and while the first impression is one of chaos, closer examination reveals that quite a considerable amount of musical information is, in fact, contained in the score.

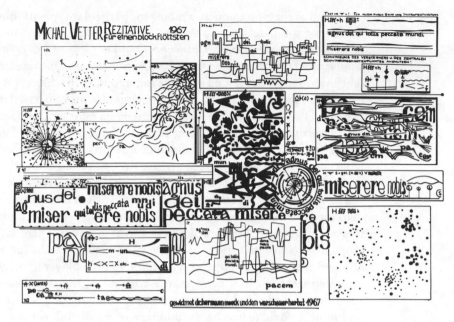

18   Michael Vetter, *Rezitative* (actual size 54 × 38 cm)

Unlike *RARA*, where there were few visual correspondences between the symbols and the type of sound they represented, in *Rezitative* the dominant graphic elements of dots, straight and curved lines and geometric patterns may be translated fairly easily into pitches and note-durations by the addition of a vertical axis of pitch and a horizontal axis of time to each field. The lettering and words are taken from the Latin *Agnus Dei* and form a text which is spoken and sung by the player. A suitable sequence for performance of the material is obtained by assigning a number to each of the eighteen fields (Vetter suggests a suitable numbering sequence) and small symbols contained in each of these fields denote the recorder or part of the recorder that is to be used, the dynamics, and the manner of manipulating the electronic equipment. Once again, full use can be made of all the new instrumental techniques, but Vetter's conception of the work calls for something more than just a display of technique. The recorder is to be used, not merely as an instrument which is 'played upon', but as a means of extending the player's own physical resources.

The virtuosity of Vetter's performances of this work attracted much attention in the late 1960s and early 1970s. His 1969 recording of *Rezitative* gives an indication of the range of his technique. The breath is used for singing and speech as well as for playing, the mouth for tongue-clicks, sucking and lip-smacking noises as well as for all the more usual forms of articulation, the hands for percussive tapping and banging sounds on the body of the instrument as well as on the finger-holes and, above all, hands as well as feet manipulate the controls of the electronic equipment. The resultant dramatic impact on the audience of this display of virtuosity is considerable.

A further point of interest is the deliberate conflict between the title, which implies something spoken or sung (a recitative), and the sub-title ('for one recorder player'), which implies something played on an instrument. The use of a text in a work for one instrumentalist is something of a contradiction in terms in any case and the choice of the *Agnus Dei* here, loaded as it inevitably is with religious connotations, is particularly curious since it is a 'hidden' text which in all its appearances except one (in field 8) is rendered unintelligible by electronic transformation. In fact, Vetter, in his introduction to the piece, specifically forbids any mention of the *Agnus Dei* in programme notes, etc. so that the audience is not led into making any assumptions about the music before it has been performed.

Nowadays, nearly twenty years after it was written, *Rezitative* is no longer performed and indeed it is doubtful if anyone but the composer himself ever has or ever could perform it. In this sense it may be said to have been a failure, in that it has not withstood the test of time. As an example of the use of avant-garde techniques in an indeterminate and improvisatory context, however, as well as of the use of live electronics, *Rezitative* is of the greatest significance as a milestone in the development of the modern repertoire.

ELECTRO-ACOUSTIC MUSIC

The recorder was first used in electro-acoustic music in the 1960s when Michael Vetter began to experiment with amplification. Since that time, with the development of the synthesiser and the increasing sophistication of sound systems, coupled with the recognition of the very individual sound-palette offered by the recorder, other composers and players have become interested in using it in electro-acoustic music.* Direct amplification of the recorder through a normal standing microphone has been used for some time to increase the volume and enhance the tone of a gentle instrument, as well as to add 'presence' and create an integrated sound when recorders are mixed with other acoustic or electronic instruments. An example of amplification used to add 'presence' is seen in *Passacaglia* (1983) for three bass recorders by Jeff Hamburg (b. 1956), where it enhances the instrumental attack. There are now many more exotic possibilities. The complexity of the technology is such

---

* In this study the term 'electro-acoustic music' is used as a general description of all forms of music which involve taped and/or electronic sound sources. Strictly speaking, the term 'electronic music' should be applied only to those works in which the music derives entirely from electronic sound sources.

as to make this into a whole new field of study outside the scope of this volume, but a brief resumé can be given here.

Electro-acoustic pieces can be divided loosely into those that use pre-recorded material on tape and those using 'live' electronic effects. In the first category the taped material consists in the majority of cases of the sound of another recorder or recorders juxtaposed with the live performance but there are a few examples in which the tape contains a sound-source other than recorders. Two compositions by Jacques Bank can be cited: *Blind Boy Fuller no. 1*, which uses the taped voice of the eponymous jazz singer, and *Maraens Trompetten* for two alto recorders and tape, in which the recorders are amplified and accompanied by a tape of loud organ pedal-notes.

One of the earliest works in the first category was *Gesten* (1966) for recorder player and tape by the German composer Klaus Hashagen (b. 1924), in which the tape assumes the role of partner to the recorder player, taking the place of the traditional keyboard accompaniment. The tape contains all sorts of superimposed recorder sounds, occasionally using echo, tape-speed changes, etc. but no electronic modification, and these sounds are contrasted with the live sounds generated by a whole battery of different recorders and sections of dismantled recorders, some of them prepared by a slight displacement of the block (Ex. 19). The 'gestures' of the title refer both to the physical actions of the performer in changing from one instrument to another, and to the musical gestures, the mixture of 'remembered' sounds on tape and 'real' sounds from the soloist. Another and similar work is *Notturno* for one bass recorder player, tape and two gongs by Martin Gümbel (p. 67), where a tape of instrumental and vocal sounds from a large group of recorder players is used as the background for the soloist.

A far more simple use of taped material occurs in *Recorder Music* for

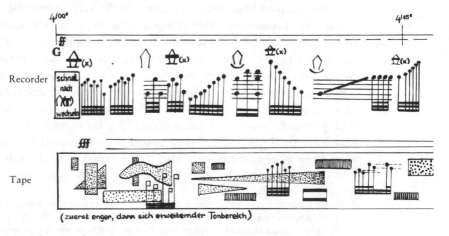

19   Klaus Hashagen, *Gesten*

recorder and tape by Peter Dickinson. Here the tape, which contains an accompanying melody, simply takes the place of a second performer (the composition can also be played without the tape in a version for two recorders). A further instance of this sort of straightforward use of the tape recorder solely as a convenient vehicle for the storage and retrieval of sound occurs in *Consort Music I* (1976) for recorder and orchestra by Herman Rechberger. In this work the opening passage, a cadenza for solo recorder, is taped at the start of the performance and played back as a counterpoint to a repeat of the same cadenza at the end of the work.

The second category, that of works using live electronics, is the more interesting in that it offers the greatest potential for the further development of the recorder in contemporary music. Michael Vetter's compositions, *Figurationen III* and *Rezitative* (p. 75) were the first of these and were innovatory in their day. The introduction of the recorder into the vanguard of contemporary music continued when Vetter began to give performances on recorder of Stockhausen's electro-acoustic piece, *Spiral*.

At about this time the Dutch composer Peter Schat (b. 1935) wrote a work entitled *Hypothema* (1969) for Frans Brüggen. This combines 'old' music, i.e. a set of van Eyck variations for soprano recorder pre-recorded on tape, and 'new' music, i.e. musical material based on a note-row and played (live) on a tenor recorder. This was the first 'interactive' piece for recorder, with both the taped and live sounds subjected to live electronic modification which is only partially under the control of the player. Events are therefore not entirely predictable and every performance will be different.

During the 1970s, electro-acoustic technology became increasingly sophisticated and composers had more scope to develop new ideas. Works such as *Sequence* (1977) for recorder and synthesiser by László Dubrovay (b. 1943) and *Canto Llano* (1978) for recorder and tape delay by Eduard Marturet (b. 1956) are good examples. The latter in particular is a simple but very beautiful piece gaining its effect from the delayed playback of successive layers of sound picked up by the electronic apparatus.

Several of today's foremost professional players believe that the future of the recorder lies in electro-acoustic music and are increasingly devoting their attention to the new technology. Recently-developed synthesisers can produce extremely complex effects under very sensitive control with the minimum of hardware. In the vanguard of the investigation of these new sounds is Michael Barker (b. 1951), an American long resident in the Netherlands and a professor at the Royal Conservatory in The Hague. Barker has developed a sophisticated system linking a square Paetzold contrabass recorder in F to two computer-controlled synthesisers. This he terms an Interactive MIDI Performance System, or 'midified blockflute'. By means of pressure-pads fitted to the undersides of the keys and a breath-sensitive membrane in the windway measuring the velocity and volume of the player's

9   Recorders don't have to be cylindrical! Herbert Paetzold and his ingenious square contrabass recorder, designed on the organ-pipe principle. The simple mechanism, particularly the large, flat keys, can be successfully modified for use in electronic music.

breath he is able, via the MIDI language (Musical Instrument Digital Interface) and the dedicated microcomputer, to mix 'real' and synthesised sounds as he plays. The reason for choosing this type of recorder for the prototype was principally that the size and design lend themselves to an experiment of this kind, coupled with the fact that the range of multiphonics available is unusually good and stable. The next stage will endeavour to develop the electronic apparatus so that it monitors the total internal environment of the recorder as it is being played, i.e. node movement, finger movement, soundwaves, etc. and transforms it instantaneously (or at any rate so quickly as to appear instantaneous) into an enormous range of sounds depending on how the computer is programmed. This 'real-time synthesis within an interactive environment', in the language of electro-acoustics, will have no element of unpredictability or randomness. It will be a completely self-generating system in that the only sounds will be either the normal, blown sounds of the recorder or their live transformations and the player will have full control over both instrument and electronics at all times.

Barker and others feel that this provides a genuine extension of the recorder and offers great possibilities for new compositional ideas. It makes it possible to obtain live electronic effects from a 'real' instrument played by a 'real' performer in front of an audience, obviating the need for long preparatory hours in a recording studio and the consequent loss of spontaneity when the prepared material is integrated in performance. Barker's system therefore has a considerable advantage, he feels, even over recent technological developments such as the Yamaha WX7, a MIDI-controlled synthesiser operated by the breath and able to be programmed to feel and sound like any wind instrument including, of course, recorder.

The next few years should show whether the promise of electro-acoustics is fulfilled. Those involved in the field are realistic enough to know that sophisticated equipment does not of itself produce good music. There must be a convincing compositional reason to use electronics, but the possibilities are certainly exciting.

7   Modern techniques

One of the most significant developments in twentieth-century music has been the expansion in instrumental techniques that led to a reassessment of the capabilities of all instruments. The concept of *Klangfarbenmelodie* ('melody of tone colours'), which made its first appearance in Schoenberg's *Five Pieces for Orchestra* of 1908, was further developed in the music of Webern, Bartók and Messiaen and can be seen as a desire on the part of composers for new sounds and hitherto unknown possibilities for expression. Since the Second World War, and since the 1960s in particular, further expansions of instrumental technique have taken place as players and composers explored the hitherto latent possibilities of their instruments.

It is not surprising that this should have happened with the more common instruments. Nowadays, however, every instrument has its vocabulary of new sounds. The trombone and double bass, for instance, which have traditionally played somewhat limited roles in the orchestra, have demonstrated a surprising capacity for originality in contemporary music. Performers such as Gary Carr, Barry Guy and Bertram Turetzky have commissioned and performed many new works for double bass and Turetzky's study of avant-garde bass techniques (Turetzky 1974) is a revelation in its range and variety of effects. Stuart Dempster, Vinko Globokar and others have similarly raised the status and level of technical expertise required of trombone players and here again the range of new techniques available, many of them originating in jazz, is impressive (Dempster 1979).

The publication of Bruno Bartolozzi's important book, *New Sounds for Woodwind* (Bartolozzi 1967), was the first major recognition of the emancipation of the woodwinds. Subsequent extensive investigations of flute fingerings (Howell 1974; Dick 1975) and clarinet fingerings (Rehfeld 1977) revealed an enormous variety of new sounds. As far as the woodwinds are concerned, and this includes the recorder, two fundamental tenets must now be reassessed in the light of these discoveries. The first is the belief that there is only one possible fingering for each note on a woodwind instrument, and the second is that woodwind instruments can play only one note at a time.

Modern techniques

Neither of these statements is true and the realisation that new fingering combinations can produce single and multiple sounds with a variety of different timbres and intonations has been perhaps the most significant event since the design innovations of the early eighteenth century gave us the prototypes of the instruments we play today. Along with the discovery of the new sound-world of non-standard fingerings has come a realisation of the possibilities offered by various forms of articulation and vibrato and of a whole panoply of special effects, some of which take the player into territory very far removed from that of conventional wind technique.

New developments in recorder technique began to be seen at very much the same time as similar developments in other instruments. Michael Vetter began his researches into non-standard fingerings in the early 1960s and his book, *Il Flauto Dolce ed Acerbo*, was published in 1969, two years after the publication of Bartolozzi's book but, interestingly, well ahead of similar treatises on other instruments such as those already mentioned. Since that time, further investigations of recorder fingerings have been undertaken by Rechberger (1987) and Kientzy (1982) but up to now there has been no attempt to categorise and document all the other equally important recorder techniques which have proliferated in the past twenty years.

Through a wide-ranging search of scores, I have sought to identify and

Group 1
Non-standard fingerings
   Single sounds:
      dynamic variation
      timbre variation
      harmonics
      microtones
   Multiphonics

Group 2
Articulation
   Single tonguing
   Double and triple tonguing
   Flutter-tonguing

Group 3
Vibrato
   Diaphragm
   Throat
   Tongue
   Finger
   Labium
   Knee

Group 4
Special effects
   Glissando
   Rustle tones
   White noise
   Random finger-play
   Percussive effects
   Circular breathing
   Vocal effects
   Mouth sounds
   Structural alterations to the instrument:
      modifications to the windway and labium
      modifications to the pipe
      foot-joint removed
      head-joint removed
      foot-joint alone
      head-joint alone
   Two recorders, one player

Fig. 3 Extended recorder techniques

classify these, with the addition of some further possibilities that have suggested themselves and for which there are as yet no suitable musical examples. Simplicity and ease of reference were a priority and the classification has been centred on the following elements of technique: fingering, tonguing, breathing and the structural conformation of the instrument itself. There are four main groups: 1, Non-standard fingering; 2, Articulation; 3, Vibrato; 4, Special effects. Within each sub-group numerous small variations of the basic technique are, of course, possible but it seemed unnecessary to document complexities which players and composers may be expected to discover for themselves. Rather the intention has been to reduce the classification to essentials.

In all cases the technique in question has been assigned to the most obvious category. All six forms of vibrato, for example, are grouped together even though their methods of production are quite different, and glissando and random finger-play are grouped with 'special effects' even though a case might be made for including them in Group 1. There is as yet no consensus on the notation of many techniques in contemporary music and no attempt has been made here to impose a standard notation which is better arrived at in due course by a process of natural selection. A good working knowledge of conventional recorder technique is assumed. Readers who find themselves at a loss in this respect are recommended to read the relevant sections of Walter van Hauwe's excellent technical manual, *The Modern Recorder Player*, vols. 1 and 2 (1984; 1987). For non-standard fingerings readers are referred to the tables in the Appendix (p. 127) of the present volume.

GROUP 1   NON-STANDARD FINGERINGS

The standard fingering system of the recorder is designed so as to give a sound that is uniformly graded in terms of pitch, tone-colour and dynamics throughout the full range of the instrument. In contemporary music, however, this homogeneity of texture and timbre becomes only one of several tone-colours in the composer's sound palette and the range of new sounds available from non-standard fingerings provides an important addition to recorder technique. Non-standard fingerings* on the recorder are classified as belonging to one of three 'registers', based on the discovery that the recorder behaves in a different manner acoustically when the end-hole is obstructed either partially or wholly. This has the effect of altering the wave

---

* 'Non-standard fingering: this term is used in preference to 'alternative fingering' or 'special fingering', since the last two terms seem to imply, incorrectly, a very specific usage of these fingerings which is rarely the case in practice. In fact, the player makes his or her choice according to individual convenience and suitability from what may be as many as twenty or thirty possible fingerings for one note.

formations within the pipe and hence the timbre of the sound produced. The three registers are designated as follows: the normal or 'open' register when the end-hole is open and the wave formation within the pipe is that of a cylinder open at both ends; the 'closed' register when the end-hole is tightly stopped, and the 'covered' register when the end-hole is obstructed but not sealed, thus encouraging the formation of a node at the end-hole. The closed register can be obtained by sealing the end-hole with a cork or plug, or by pressing the end of the recorder against a piece of thick plastic secured to the knee. The 'covered' register can be obtained by lightly pressing the end-hole against the clothing on the knee or by pushing a piece of soft cloth into it. The methods chosen must depend on the context and particularly on the amount of time available to switch to and from normal sound production (see also p. 112).

It has been estimated (Rechberger 1987, 8) that there are as many as 6,500 different fingering combinations available on the open register of the recorder if three possible conformations of each finger-hole are taken into account, i.e. open, half-closed, closed. Add to this the same number of fingerings on the other two registers also and the total reaches something in the region of 20,000. Not all of these fingerings are viable on every recorder but a very sizeable proportion of them produce useful single and multiple sounds of varying timbre and dynamic level as well as upward and downward extensions of the normal range. Many notes of the recorder have thirty or forty viable alternatives to the standard fingering in the open register alone, and some have more. Vetter, for instance, lists seventy-nine non-standard fingerings in the open register for *b'''* flat, a further forty-seven fingerings for the same note in the closed register and twenty-seven in the covered register (Vetter 1969).

Non-standard fingerings may be divided into two main types. The first type consists of those which produce single sounds* and may be subdivided into fingerings which give: 1, dynamic variation; 2, timbre variation; 3, harmonics; 4, microtones. The second type consists of those non-standard fingerings which give multiple sounds, known as multiphonics. The latter may be made up of two, three or more simultaneous sounds in varying degrees of prominence and are subject to the same variations of tone and timbre as single sounds. Such variations are, however, more difficult to describe with precision in the case of multiphonics and are not, therefore, treated here under separate subheadings. All non-standard fingerings require good coordination of breathing and fingering and because many are less stable than their standard-fingered counterparts, allowance must be made for this when using them in a composition.

---

* The term 'single sound' or 'monophonic' is used to describe those notes that we normally hear as such, although they are in fact made up of a fundamental plus a group of related harmonics. This is to distinguish them from multiphonics, which are heard as a collection of discrete, frequently dissonant, pitches.

Single sounds

Dynamic variation

Variations in the dynamic level of a note are obtained by altering the normal relationship of fingering to breath pressure. Because increasing or decreasing breath pressure affects the tuning as well as the volume of the note, a change of dynamics is achieved by choosing a non-standard fingering that is slightly out-of-tune and then making a compensatory adjustment in breath pressure. Thus, loud notes are played by choosing a 'flat' fingering and blowing more than normal so that the note sounds in tune but louder, and soft notes are played by choosing a 'sharp' fingering and blowing less than normal. 'Soft' and 'loud' fingerings are generally chosen from the open register and are closely related to the standard fingerings in that the pattern of closed and open holes is similar (Ex. 20).

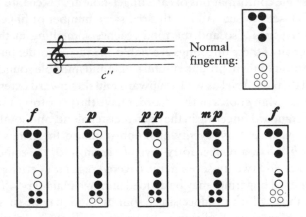

20 Non-standard fingerings for dynamic variation (1)

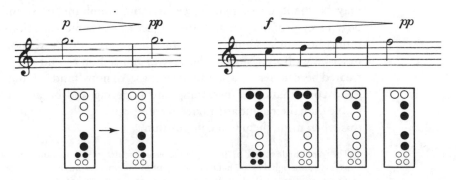

21 Non-standard fingerings for dynamic variation (2). After Rechberger (1987)

Modern techniques

Crescendos and decrescendos obtained with non-standard fingerings can be very effective but allowance must be made for the awkwardness of many fingering sequences. It is not realistic, for instance, to expect a whole passage of rapid notes to be played using non-standard fingerings. In general, it is wiser to restrict large dynamic changes to single, sustained notes or to slow passages where the effect is more telling. On a sustained note a smooth crescendo and decrescendo can be obtained by sliding one finger on and off a finger-hole while altering the breath pressure accordingly, so that the dynamic level changes but the pitch remains constant (Ex. 21).

Timbre variation

The characteristic timbre of a musical sound derives from the composition of the group of upper harmonics which accompanies the fundamental. Playing the same note with different fingerings has the effect of changing the composition of the group of harmonics and hence the timbre of the sound. Non-standard fingerings can therefore be used to obtain various different timbres. A very simple illustration of timbre variation is shown in Ex. 22 where the standard fingering for g'' flat is alternated with a non-standard fingering A similar device is used by Heider in *Katalog* (Ex. 23). As in the case of dynamic variations, the fingerings for timbre variations are generally taken from the open register and again, the practicalities of the finger movements must be taken into consideration.

22   Hans-Martin Linde, *Music for a Bird*, no. 4

23   Werner Heider, *Katalog*

87

Harmonics

Although in the strictest sense all the notes of the recorder are harmonics
except for the seven fundamental tones (see Chapter 3, p. 27), the term
'harmonic' or sometimes 'flageolet tone', is used in recorder music to describe
a very specific type of weak, underblown sound which is sometimes so soft as
to be virtually inaudible. In general the fingering for a harmonic is similar to
that of the normal tone but with one or more finger-holes, usually the thumb-
hole, 'leaking' or half open. The resulting sound is then a single harmonic
rather than a complex group of upper harmonics. Breath pressure for
harmonics is considerably less than normal, and some harmonics are very
unstable. They can be highly effective, however, especially when a particularly soft, ethereal sound is called for, as in Ex. 24 and Ex. 25.

Recorder harmonics are notated in the usual way ($\overset{\circ}{\rho}$), or by the designation 'flag.' or 'harm.' over the passage in question. Both Rechberger and
Vetter list recorder harmonics in the open register in the range *f'* sharp to
d''', although it should be said that *f'*, *b''* and *c'''* cannot be played as
harmonics. Harmonics are also available in the closed and covered registers.
In the case of the closed register the notes *e'* flat, *d'* and *b* flat are available,
thus providing a useful downward extension of the range.

flag. /ord.
unregelmäßig wechseln
[harmonic/normal tone –
alternate irregularly]

24   Gerhard Braun, *Monologe I*

25   Rob du Bois, *Pastorale VII*

Microtones

It is one of the advantages of the recorder that, because of the absence of keys,
microtones can be played with accuracy by modifying the standard fingerings. Microtones are usually produced by fractionally opening or closing one

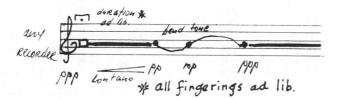

26 Walter Hekster, *Encounter*

27 Makoto Shinohara, *Fragmente*

28 John Casken, *Thymehaze*

or more of the finger-holes of the standard fingering, but occasionally it is necessary to add or subtract fully open or closed finger-holes. It is also possible to effect microtonal changes in pitch by using standard fingerings with increased or decreased breath pressure. These 'bent tones', as they are called by jazz musicians, are used on sustained notes such as those in Ex. 26, whereas in a passage such as that in Ex. 27, non-standard fingerings should be used to ensure accuracy of pitch. Microtonal glissandos may be effected by gradually sliding or rolling the fingers on and off the finger-holes (Ex. 28).

Multiphonics

On all wind instruments certain non-standard fingerings will produce multiphonics and these have now become accepted by composers and players as a

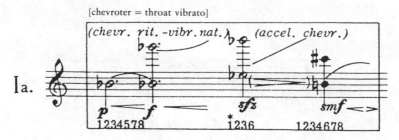

29 Jürg Baur, *Mutazioni*: © Breitkopf & Härtel, Wiesbaden

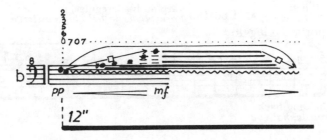

30 Kazimierz Serocki, *Arrangements*, no. 4

valid addition to modern technique. Opinions vary as to the exact acoustical origin of these sounds but it appears that they are the result of the oscillation of a group of frequencies which are not part of the same harmonic series and which cannot therefore be rationalised by the ear into a single sound. Some multiphonics consist of two or three strong, identifiable pitches, others consist of a complex group of sounds in varying degrees of prominence whose separate components are almost impossible to isolate and identify without the aid of electronic apparatus. Multiphonics are more difficult to play than single sounds; they are less stable and require a high degree of breath control as well as a keen sense of pitch in order to initiate and sustain the sounds. They are available in the open, closed and covered registers and, like single sounds, may be selected for their individual qualities of dynamics and timbre, although these will vary with different instruments and players. There are also considerable differences in the results when the same multiphonic fingering is applied to the various members of the recorder family. Bass recorders are a particularly rich source of multiphonics.

The examples cited show some of the ways in which multiphonics can be used. Ex. 29 is one of the variations from Baur's semi-improvisatory serial piece for solo alto recorder, *Mutazioni*, showing the suggested interpretation of this movement as given in Vetter's performing edition. Ex. 30 is an excerpt for bass recorder from *Arrangements* by Kazimierz Serocki (1922–81). These examples serve as some indication of how dynamics, vibrato and articulation can be applied to a multiphonic passage to enhance its effect.

GROUP 2   ARTICULATION

The primary source of articulation in recorder playing is the tongue, which, by forming one of a number of possible attack and release syllables, gives an important colour and shape to the sounds. Articulation plays an important role in the interpretation of modern recorder music and in recent compositions the tendency is for composers to be quite specific in notating it. Single, double and triple tonguing are, of course, part of the normal technique of any woodwind instrument, but increasingly, composers and players are using these methods of articulation in new ways. Flutter-tonguing is a relatively new technique.

In the interpretation of articulation syllables, language differences should be taken into consideration and the player will find it useful to think about the composer's native language sounds before attempting to put the instructions into practice.

Single tonguing

The standard articulation sounds for single tonguing are 'd' and 't'. Both use the tip of the tongue and sounds can be played in a variety of ways ranging from legato to staccato. Some extreme variants of these tonguing sounds are shown below. The syllable 'td' (not to be confused with the double tonguing syllables 't-d' below) produces a short, accented note with beginning and ending clearly defined (Ex. 31). The hard, 'quasi pizzicato' tonguing in Ex. 32 is

31   Werner Heider, *Katalog*

32   Hans-Martin Linde, *Music for a Bird*, no. 6

91

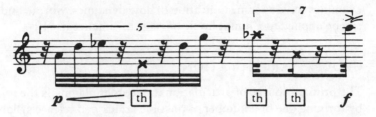

33   Konrad Lechner, *Spuren im Sand*, no. 11

34   Konrad Lechner, *Varianti* I, no. 2

35   Rolf Riehm, *Gebräuchliches*

36   Konrad Lechner, *Varianti* I, no. 2

open-ended. A sharp articulation sound mixed with air noise results when the German 'th' is used (Ex. 33). This is played with the mouth slightly open and a distinct 'h' follows the initial 't'. It is a good example of a possible source of linguistic confusion: the English 'th' as in *Theme* ('thihm') is quite different from the 'th' sound as in *Thema* ('tay'mah') in German and other European languages. Examples 34 and 35 call for two articulation sounds that do not involve a movement of the tongue – these are 'h' and 'p'. A very short and forceful form of articulation known as 'sputato' tonguing (Ex. 36) is obtained by positioning the tongue against the hard palate and forcing the air into the recorder with an explosive 'di' sound. By this means the resultant sound is almost entirely dominated by the attack consonant with the actual content of pitched sound reduced to a minimum.

Double and triple tonguing

Double tonguing uses a rapidly alternating movement of the tongue as in pronouncing the sounds 't-d', 'd-r', 't-k', etc., thus enabling a fast passage to be articulated distinctly at speeds that would be too great for single tonguing (Ex. 37). Triple tonguing is used to articulate fast passages, which fall into patterns of threes. Here the customary articulation sounds include 't-d-r', 't-k-t', etc. In Ex. 38 the rapid articulation is accompanied by a roughening of the sound caused by overblowing towards the top note.

37   Konrad Lechner, *Spuren im Sand*, no. 4

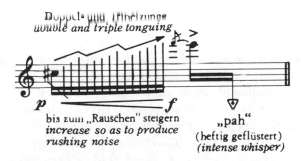

38   Konrad Lechner, *Varianti* I, no. 3

Flutter-tonguing

The rolled 'r' produced by the tip of the tongue gives an effect known to all wind players as 'flutter-tonguing' (*Flatterzunge, frullato*). The effect is that of a rapid, regular fluttering or vibration of the note. Flutter-tonguing is highly effective on the recorder and is frequently used in contemporary works (Ex. 39).

There are a number of variants of flutter sounds, one of which is used by Braun in *Minimal Music II*. This he terms 'Flatterlippe' and describes it as

93

[Flz.: flutter-tonguing]

39   Rob du Bois, *Muziek*

ganze Flöte / whole recorder

Flatterzunge   (1234 67)
[Flutter-tonguing]

Flatterlippe
Flutter-lip

40   Gerhard Braun, *Minimal Music II*

being produced when air is directed into the space between the upper lip and the upper teeth (Ex. 40).

GROUP 3   VIBRATO

Vibrato is one of the most important means available to the recorder player of achieving varying tone-colour, intensity, dynamics and pitch. The question of whether vibrato should be a constant element of recorder tone or whether it should be used only as a decorative device has already been discussed but so far as contemporary recorder music is concerned it may be said that its use is not automatic but is left to the discretion of the performer according to the context. Where a particular effect is desired, as in the examples shown below, it is specified by the composer. Occasionally the use of vibrato is specifically forbidden.

Apart from the standard diaphragm vibrato used by all woodwind players, at least five other types of vibrato can be identified.

Diaphragm vibrato

As in standard woodwind technique, the action of the diaphragm in recorder playing creates an oscillation of pitch on either side of the note which may be produced at varying speeds and intensities. In general, diaphragm vibrato is only referred to in a score when the composer has something exceptional in mind. Exx. 41 and 42 show two such instances.

94

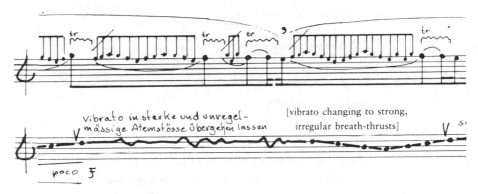

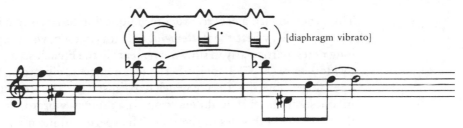

41   Martin Gümbel, *Flötenstories* I, no. 2

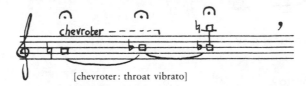

42   Konrad Lechner, *Spuren im Sand*, no. 8

Throat vibrato

This, the so-called 'goat's trill', is a rapid, regular oscillation in the throat caused by a constriction of the air-flow as in an unvoiced 'ha ha ha' (Ex. 43). It is relatively easy to produce but cannot be controlled and varied in the same degree as diaphragm vibrato. Throat vibrato is also known by the French term 'chevroter'.

[chevroter: throat vibrato]

43   Rob du Bois, *Pastorale VII*

Tongue vibrato

This is a rapid tongue movement, as in saying 'lu lu lu lu' while the note is being played (Ex. 44). The movement of the tongue inside the mouth inter-

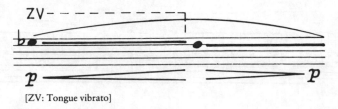

[ZV: Tongue vibrato]

44   Hans-Martin Linde, *Märchen*, no. 3

feres with the flow of air into the instrument and causes a slight fluctuation in the intensity of the note. This technique is not often used.

Finger vibrato

This is not, in fact, a new recorder technique, but has its origin in eighteenth-century music, where the *flattement*, as it was known, was used to embellish long notes, particularly in slow movements in the French style. It is described by Hotteterre (1707) among others and is a fingered vibrato on the edge of an open finger-hole, the effect of which is to cause a flattening of pitch of the note in question. In this it differs from diaphragm vibrato, in which pitch fluctuates on both sides of the note. The speed and intensity of the vibrato may be varied by the action of the finger on the finger-hole (Ex. 45). Finger vibrato is not available on the lowest note of the recorder because to play this note all finger-holes are closed. In this instance the solution suggested by Hotteterre for producing an acceptable imitation of finger vibrato may be adopted, that is, waving the end of the recorder slightly.

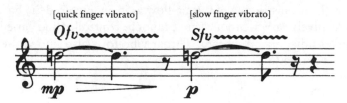

[quick finger vibrato]   [slow finger vibrato]

45   Rob du Bois, *Muziek*

Labium vibrato

Covering the labium with one cupped hand has the effect of lowering the pitch and a vibrato may be obtained (on the flat side of the note) by moving the right hand over the aperture while fingering with the thumb and first three fingers of the left hand. In Ex. 46 the *d''* flat and the vibrato are obtained by shading the labium with the right hand in this manner. The diminuendo effect is obtained at the same time by carefully coordinating the diminishing

96

Modern techniques

[Labium vibrato]

46 Hans-Martin Linde, *Music for a Bird*, no. 2

p e *dolce*

[Labium vibrato]

47 Hans-Martin Linde, *Music for a Bird*, no. 6

airstream and the degree of shading. A slow vibrato such as that seen in Ex. 47 is particularly effective.

Knee vibrato

A vibrato effect may also be obtained by shading the end-hole of the instrument on the player's knee. The resultant vibrato is on the flat side of the note and has a more noticeable effect on high notes than on lower ones (Ex. 48).

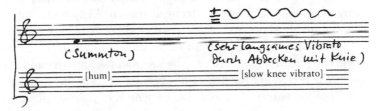

(Summton)

(Sehr langsames Vibrato durch Abdecken mit Knie)

[hum]   [slow knee vibrato]

48 Hans-Martin Linde, *Consort Music*, third movement

GROUP 4 SPECIAL EFFECTS

Glissando

A recorder glissando is played by sliding the fingers on or off the finger-holes in such a way as to close or open the apertures gradually and consecutively. The absence of keywork on the recorder means that there is no sudden inter-

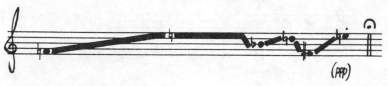

49   Rob du Bois, *Pastorale VII*

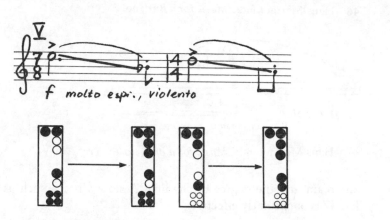

50   Roland Moser, *Alrune*

ruption in the pitch gradient, and if the player is listening carefully, glissandos such as those shown in Ex. 49 may be executed very smoothly.

Although not always necessary, the use of non-standard fingerings some-times simplifies glissando passages. In Ex. 50, for instance, the non-standard fingerings suggested for the first note of each glissando reduce the number of fingers involved in the change to two or three instead of four or five.

Glissandos starting or finishing on microtones can be played with a high degree of accuracy, limited only by the manual dexterity and aural sensitivity of the player, since the degree of aperture of each finger-hole and hence the pitch of the note, can be adjusted very minutely by the placing of the fingers on the edge of the finger-holes (Ex. 51). A glissando cannot be played across a register break (such as those between *g''* and *a''*, *d'''* and *e'''* and *f'''* and *g'''*, for instance) because here the fingering pattern requires a change from opening finger-holes to closing them. Non-standard fingerings can generally be found which will produce a smooth pitch gradient in these cases.

Glissandos are usually notated with a line joining the lowest and highest notes, as in the examples above, and the realisation of the fingering is left up to the player. Another form of notation shows the action of the fingers rather than the pitch of the notes. This type of notation is appropriate in a context such as that of Ex. 52, where the glissando is part of a graphically-notated opening recorder cadenza.

13. ♭E

51   Makoto Shinohara, *Fragmente*

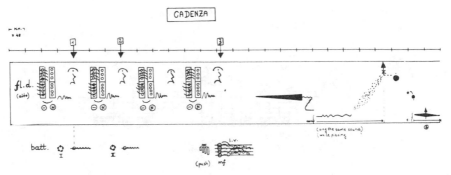

52   Herman Rechberger, *Consort Music I*

Rustle tones

Distorting or in some way impeding the air supply to the instrument results in what are known as rustle tones or breathy tones, that is, muted notes accompanied by air noise. One way of doing this is to hold the mouthpiece loosely between the lips or in the corner of the mouth so that some of the air escapes around it. Alternatively, the instrument may be rested at a vertical or near-vertical angle against the bottom lip and the airstream directed across the top of the windway with the lips pursed as in flute playing. The latter method has the advantage that rustle sounds can be blended without a break into normal, pitched sounds by raising the recorder and gradually closing the lips around the mouthpiece in the usual way. The mixture of normal tone and noise in a rustle tone varies according to the articulation used. A hard 't' articulation, for instance, or an 'f' or 'fht' articulation, produces a sharp air noise at the beginning of the sound. By contrast, the 'breathy flutter tongue' used by du Bois in *Muziek* (Ex. 53) gives a soft, rustling sound accompanying the instrumental sound.

When rustle tones are mixed with rapid double tonguing, as in Ex. 54, because the airstream is directed across rather than into the windway, the articulation consonants and the whistling of the air are heard quite distinctly as accompaniment to the fingered pitches which are sounded softly but

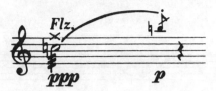

[Flz.: Flutter-tonguing with audible breath noise]
×

53   Rob du Bois, *Muziek*

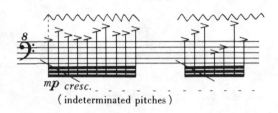

(indeterminated pitches)

   set the instrument to lips as below. "TKTK" is tonguing indication without utterance and fingering is the same as usual

54   Ryohei Hirose, *Lamentation*

normally. In Japanese-influenced pieces such as *Lamentation* and *Meditation* by Hirose, rustle tones are used to suggest the sound of the shakuhachi. Players will find that infinite subtle variations are possible with this technique.

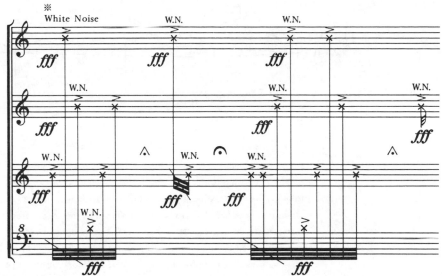

※ すべての指穴をふさぎ，さらに足部管の下穴をひざに押し当てて閉じ，吹口に息を強く吹き込む。
Overblow with all finger holes and register covered (placing the recorder on the knee to close lower opening).

55   Ryohei Hirose, *Lamentation*

White noise

This is an acoustical term describing any noise which is composed of sounds encompassing a broad frequency spectrum and in which no single frequency, and therefore pitch, predominates. Recorder players will be familiar with one form of white noise as the sound they hear when they cover the labium with a finger and blow into the mouthpiece to clear a blocked windway. Several variants of this harsh, hissing or whistling air noise are obtainable, their pitch range depending on the way they are produced and, of course, the size of the recorder. Methods of production include overblowing while covering all finger-holes and the end-hole (Ex. 55); overblowing while covering the labium with the fingers, the pitch and quality of the sound depending on how tightly the fingers close the window; blowing into or across the labium as into a flute mouthpiece with the recorder held transversely, adjusting the pitch-band by means of the fingering; and, finally, again in the transverse position, blowing into or across any of the finger-holes (Ex. 56). The Amsterdam Loeki Stardust Quartet have devised entertaining and imaginative uses for all these methods in the rhythmic introduction to Paul Leenhouts's *Report upon 'When shall the sun shine?'* (Ex. 57).

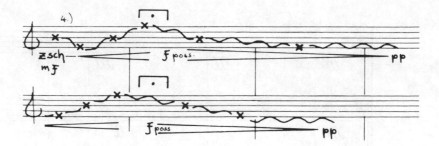

4) Hold the recorder sideway in such a manner that the left hand closes the labium while the right hand covers the lowest 3 to 4 finger-holes approximately. A whispered (i. e. non-vocal) hissing tone is now required to be produced in the tone-holes that remain uncovered. This is subjected to constant change, accomplishied by continously altering the shape of the oral cavity. The directions implied by the symbol ✗ according to its position on the staff are as follows:

= open tone-holes
close labium

= close tone-holes
and labium

= open tone-holes
and labium

56 Martin Gümbel, *Flötenstories* VI, no. 3

57 Paul Leenhouts, *Report upon 'When shall the sun shine?'*

102

Modern techniques

Random finger-play

This is a term used to describe a series of random, improvisatory finger movements, usually over a group of finger-holes corresponding to an area of pitch which may be specified to a greater or lesser degree by the composer. This technique is capable of great variety in its effect, producing a rapid succession of uncoordinated sounds which, depending on the breath pressure, may vary from soft, toneless tapping sounds to normal notes or to noisy, overblown sounds. Random finger-play is used in a number of different contexts in the modern repertoire and, as the examples demonstrate, there is no single standardised notation. In Ex. 58 Linde indicates the actions of the fingers of each hand separately. The passage shown begins very softly, below the level of breath pressure at which recognisable pitches are heard, and builds in a crescendo to *sfz*. All elements – pitch, dynamics and rhythm – are improvised within the general areas indicated by the composer. The next example (Ex. 59) is a very fast and aggressive passage in which the player improvises on the group of pitches indicated between the square brackets. The whole passage is played at high breath pressure to obtain the *fortissimo* dynamic level indicated. In Ex. 60, Hirose uses a less specific notation than that used in the two examples mentioned above. The direction given is: 'tongue as fast as possible, moving right- and left-hand fingers according to the illustrated instruction (pitches moved approximately to the illustrated instructions)'. Breath pressure is normal.

There is at first little apparent difference between this technique and that used by Andriessen in the previous example, but Hirose uses both forms of

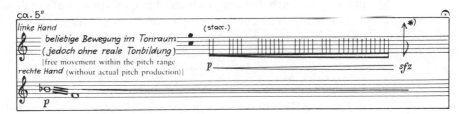

58   Hans-Martin Linde, *Amarilli mia bella*, no. 1

59   Louis Andriessen, *Sweet*

103

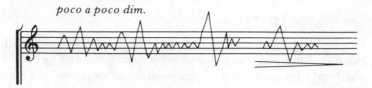

poco a poco dim.

60 Ryohei Hirose, *Lamentation*

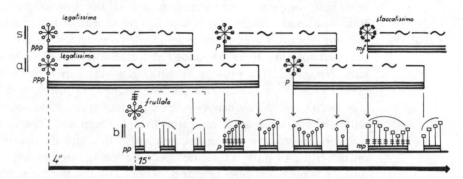

61 Kazimierz Serocki, *Arrangements*, no. 12

notation within the same composition (in *Meditation* and *Lamentation*), with the zig-zag type seen in Ex. 60 being the faster and the more improvisatory of the two.

Serocki has assigned his own system of notation to several variants of random finger-play, distinguished from one another by the level of breath pressure at which they are produced. Ex. 61 shows six of these variants in use. The notation is somewhat complex and it is questionable whether it is not over-elaborate for the purpose.

Percussive effects

In contemporary music the aim very often is not to produce a beautiful sound but rather the reverse, and composers and players have devised a variety of noise effects, some of which have already been discussed (see pp. 99–102). Tapping loudly on a finger-hole or key as the note is initiated adds a percussive element to the sound and gives an added impetus to short notes (Ex. 62). When combined with a hard, sputato tonguing it is particularly effective.

Tapping the fingers on the open holes of the recorder without blowing, or without even holding the recorder in the mouth, produces a soft, pitched percussive sound. Perhaps the best-known example of this occurs in the opening passage of Berio's *Gesti*, where the player fingers the recorder in rapid

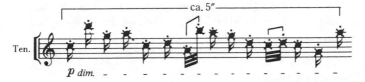

62   Maki Ishii, *Black Intention*

63   Gerhard Braun, *Schattenbilder*, no. 2

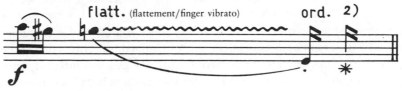

2) slap end-hole with palm of hand

64   Hans-Martin Linde, *Märchen*, no. 6

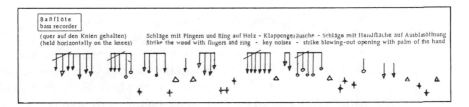

65   Gerhard Braun, *Minimal Music II*

tapping movements without blowing into the instrument. Other percussive effects include the sound of a finger-nail or of a ring on the player's finger striking the barrel of the recorder. This has the advantage of making a sharp, clearly audible sound which can be combined with a blown note fingered with the other hand, as seen in Ex. 63. A loud, hollow smacking sound can be produced by slapping the end-hole or the labium area of the recorder with the palm of the hand (Ex. 64). Further possibilities can be devised at will, as Ex. 65 suggests.

Michael Vetter has developed a technique in which the performer holds the recorder transversely between the left shoulder and the right knee, supporting it with the left hand. In this position the mouth can be placed at the window to produce a variety of blowing, tongue-clicking and lip-smacking noises (see

p. 110), and the right hand is free to make tapping and banging noises on the finger-holes, barrel and end-hole. When used with electronics a wide range of curious sounds is available.

Circular breathing

This technique, found in several folk cultures, enables the player to maintain a continuous, unbroken airstream, replenishing the air by inhaling through the nose while simultaneously exhaling through the mouth. This makes it possible to play long passages, or even whole compositions, without any of the usual breaks for exhalation and inhalation which are an otherwise inescapable feature of wind music. Contrary to the general belief, it is not necessary to have a strong resistance to the breath, such as that provided by a reed, in order to make the very quick exchange of air which allows a note to continue uninterrupted. Recorder players also can master the knack of using the cheeks to push a little spurt of air into the instrument to cover the brief moment of inhalation through the nose. This is one of the few extended techniques that most players will have genuine difficulty in mastering. The Canadian player Peter Hannan uses circular breathing in a number of his own compositions, as does the American player Pete Rose.

Vocal effects

Some very interesting effects are created on the recorder when the player sings and plays at the same time. When a hummed or sung tone is combined with a recorder note at the same pitch the sound is reinforced, but with an alteration in timbre. When the pitch of the vocal and instrumental sounds differs, combination and difference tones* arise which distort the sound, and these can be manipulated to obtain some quite bizarre results. Two fairly typical instances of the use of simultaneous singing and playing are seen in Ex. 66 and Ex. 67. A more subtle use of the voice in Ishii's *Black Intention* (Ex. 68) suggests further possibilities for the same technique, while in *Varianti*, Lechner creates an imitation of Bulgarian bagpipes by using a vocal drone as accompaniment to the instrumental sound (Ex. 69). Vocal sounds can also be combined with various different types of articulation, such as flutter-tonguing, for instance. When used with this as well as random finger-play, a distorted, noisy, very aggressive effect results (Ex. 70).

If the performer's voice is not within the range indicated by the composer, as might happen in the case of a woman playing Ex. 69 or a man Ex. 67, then

---

* These are sounds which may be heard when two notes are played together. A combination tone is formed from the sum of the frequencies and is thus a higher sound, while a difference tone is formed from the differences between the frequencies and is thus a lower sound. In both cases a third sound arises which no one is actually playing.

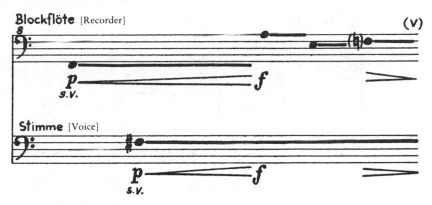

66   Hans-Martin Linde, *Amarilli mia bella*, no. 3

[m: tone with humming sound]

67   Hans-Martin Linde, *Music for a Bird*, no. 6

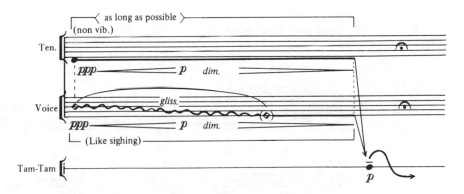

68   Maki Ishii, *Black Intention*

it is usually possible to make an appropriate octave transposition. Occasionally the composer gives special instructions about this. There are also
instances where one or other voice is preferable. In the case of Ex. 70, a loud,
deep, man's voice produces a much more impressive effect than a woman's.

When the vocal and instrumental sounds are deliberately unrelated, the
effect is one of distortion and alienation. In the example (Ex. 71) from

5 Gaida*

Presto possibile

Stimme (Summton)**
voice (hum)**

69   Konrad Lechner, *Varianti* I, no. 5

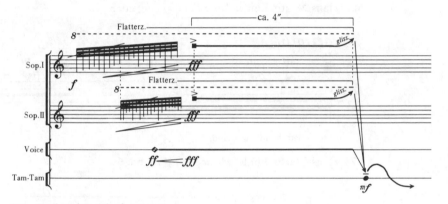

70   Maki Ishii, *Black Intention*

71   Kazimierz Serocki, *Arrangements*, no. 15

Modern techniques

Serocki's *Arrangements*, the term 'con voce' signifies just this usage and is explained by the composer as follows:

This signifies that, while blowing the prescribed note, a second note is to be sung . . . a change in the note that is blown should be accompanied by a change in the note sung. The pitch of the vocalized note should not be identical to that produced on the recorder, not even to the extent of sounding in octaves. The object of this is to create a bizarre bi-tonal effect (instrument + voice), both notes differing from each other as regards timbre and intervallic range (reminiscent of 'electronic' sound effects).

(Serocki, *Arrangements*, 1976)

Having combined hummed and sung notes with instrumental sounds, a number of composers have gone one stage further and added words to the vocal sounds. When words are spoken or sung into the recorder and mixed with blown notes their sense is, of course, lost to all but the player and the composer. The resulting sounds, however, are enriched by the vowels and consonants of the words. One of the most unusual uses of a text in recorder music has been mentioned previously. It occurs in *Rezitative* by Michael Vetter, in which the words of the *Agnus Dei* are sung and chanted, combined with taped sounds and electronic modification in such a way as to obscure its sense completely – a deliberate concealment in this case. Other composers, notably Jacques Bank, have devised other uses for words. In *Die Ouwe* (Ex. 72), Bank does not actually combine the words with the instrumental

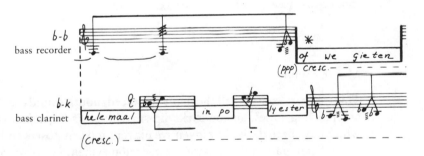

72   Jacques Bank, *Die Ouwe*

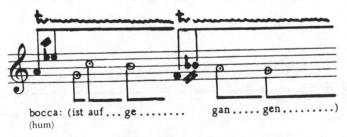

73   Gerhard Braun, *Nachtstücke*, no. 1

74 Will Eisma, *Hot, powdery stones*

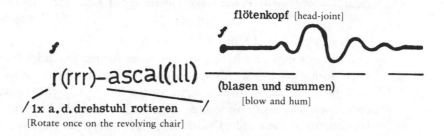

75 Klaus Hashagen, *Gardinenpredigt eines Blockflötenspielers*

© Hänssler-Verlag Neuhausen–Stuttgart

sounds but intersperses them in rapid succession without a break. Braun
(Ex. 73) requires the recorder player to hum a snatch of a song while playing
something else. Two final examples show a more light-hearted and possibly
tongue-in-cheek use of the voice (Ex. 74 and Ex. 75).

Mouth sounds

This category contains all the many unvoiced mouth sounds such as sucking
and blowing noises, tongue-clicks, lip-smacking, kissing noises, laughter, etc.
which have been devised by inventive players and composers and which form
a significant part of the theatrical dimension evident in many contemporary
recorder works. Exx. 76, 77 and 78 give some indication of the many uses of
mouth sounds, which are largely self-explanatory in their execution.

76 Gerhard Braun, *Schattenbilder*, no. 4

110

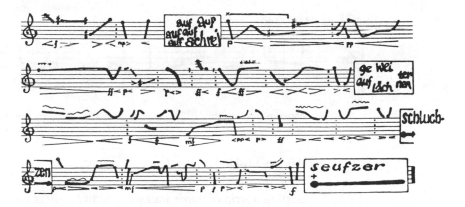

77   Sylvano Bussotti, *RARA*. Realisation by M. Vetter

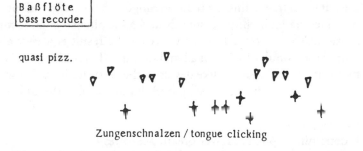

78   Gerhard Braun, *Minimal Music II*

Structural alterations to the instrument

In all the techniques so far described a normal, structurally unaltered recorder
was used. A new range of sounds is opened up by modifying or in some way
'preparing' the recorder. Such structural alterations include modifications to
the windway and labium, as well as partially or wholly dismantling the
instrument. It is important to realise that any preparation or alteration of the
instrument, such as removing one of the joints, takes time and this must be
allowed for. Most performers, however, prefer to have several instruments,
or parts of instruments, prepared beforehand and ready to use in the course
of the performance.

Modifications to the windway and labium

There is a limit to the modifications that can be made to the tone-producing
mechanism, i.e. the windway and the labium, but moving the block up or

111

※ Cover approximately two thirds of lip window with a finger tip of right hand. Play at random, using left hand fingerings for following tones;

79 Ryohei Hirose, *Idyll I*

down or inserting a strip of paper into the windway alters the timbre of the notes and stifles the tone. Loosely covering the labium lowers the overall pitch of the instrument but does not interfere with relative pitches or prevent notes from sounding. The right hand can be used to cover the labium, leaving the left hand free to finger a reduced range of pitches. Sounds produced in this way include high chirping sounds and soft, pitched sounds mixed with air noise. In Ex. 79 from *Idyll I* by Hirose the result is a very attractive soft, muted tone similar to that of a bamboo flute. This effect can also be obtained by fitting a simple shield-like device to the recorder in such a way as to cover part of the labium, thus freeing both hands to play the full compass of the instrument. Closing the labium quite tightly with the fingers gives a very high, overblown sound at high breath pressure and various noise effects of indeterminate pitch at lower breath pressures (see p. 101). A narrow strip of adhesive tape partly covering the labium, as used by Rechberger in his composition *pp* (1982), produces unpredictable distortions of the sound, particularly in the middle and upper registers.

Modifications to the pipe

A strip of rolled paper inserted in the end-hole of the recorder has a flattening effect on the lowest note. Small pieces of plasticine, blu-tack or a similar substance attached to the inside surface of the barrel near a finger-hole alters the tuning of that note. These devices are sometimes used by players to correct minor deficiencies in their instruments but they are also potentially useful in avant-garde music.

The altered response when the end-hole is closed or covered has already been discussed (see Group 1, p. 84). One further type of altered acoustical response has been mentioned by Rechberger (1987, 8). This occurs when the end-hole is closed with adhesive tape, which he claims produces a distinctly different effect from any other method of closing the end-hole, perhaps because the tape acts as a resonating membrane. The acoustical response is very distorted and unpredictable, varying considerably from one instrument

Modern techniques

to another. Reliable fingerings and notation cannot be given and it must be left to the individual player to explore the possibilities.

Foot-joint removed

Removal of the foot-joint of the recorder not only means that the lowest note cannot be played (because the finger-hole is on the bottom joint), but also affects the tuning and timbre of other notes higher in the range (Ex. 80).

12. Dreikönigsmarsch · March of the Three Kings

80   Gerhard Braun, *Minnelen der Nacht*

Head-joint removed

Removal of the head-joint has the obvious consequence of removing the means of producing a fully-developed musical note, but various other effects are still available from the barrel of the recorder. Hirose, for instance, directs the player to blow into the middle joint as if blowing across the mouth of a bottle (Ex. 81), while Braun asks the player to blow 'à la cornetto' as if into a brass mouthpiece (Ex. 82). In both cases the pitch of the resultant air-noise can be altered by opening and closing the finger-holes. Humming, singing or speaking into the pipe also produces some interesting effects.

81   Ryohei Hirose, *Lamentation*

113

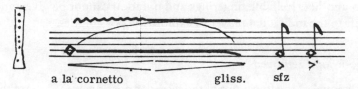

a la cornetto   gliss.   sfz

82   Gerhard Braun, *Monologe I*   © Hänssler–Verlag Neuhausen–Stuttgart

Foot-joint alone

A tenor or bass recorder foot-joint separated from the rest of the instrument is a useful source of percussive key-noises (Ex. 83).

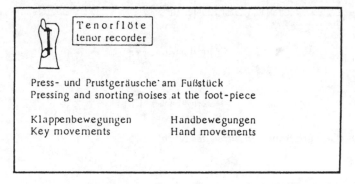

83   Gerhard Braun, *Minimal Music II*

Head-joint alone

It is only to be expected that the part of the dismantled recorder which offers the greatest range of new sounds is the head-joint. Serocki is the composer above all others who has exploited this source of new sounds. His composition *Arrangements* shows a whole panoply of special effects obtained by varying the breath-pressure, occluding or closing the labium or end-hole and using vocal effects.

Two recorders, one player

In a number of contemporary works the performer is required to play two recorders simultaneously, holding one in each hand and fingering on the thumb-hole and first three finger-holes of each, as in *Black Intention* by Ishii. The same technique has also been used by Andriessen in *Ende*, a short piece for two alto recorders which explores the sonorities of the instruments within the very close limits of the notes which can be played on the first four finger-holes, i.e. *c''*, *d''*, *e''*, *f''*, *g''* and a slightly out-of-tune *b'*. Dickinson makes a reference to the medieval double pipe in his composition, *Recorder Music*, where garkleinflötlein and sopranino recorders are played together as accompaniment to the taped sounds of a primitive folk flute.

The range of pitches available when playing two recorders together can be altered by sealing some of the finger-holes with adhesive tape, thus compensating for the shortage of fingers to cover finger-holes. This technique is used by Gümbel in *Flötenstories*. Two recorder mouthpieces may also be played at the same time and many improvisatory sound effects obtained, as in Serocki's *Concerto alla cadenza*. There is also, of course, a strong visual and dramatic element in the use of two recorders in this way.

8   Conclusions

The growth of recorder playing in the twentieth century is something that could hardly have been predicted by Arnold Dolmetsch when, in 1905, he invested the sum of £5.2s.6d. on a boxwood and ivory alto recorder at Sotheby's. Nor could anyone observing the falling fortunes of the recorder at the turn of the eighteenth century have envisaged a second chance for it at the turn of the nineteenth. That the recorder is now played in so many different musical contexts, professional and amateur, in so many parts of the world, is surely more than just a lucky accident. One must conclude that, somehow, this little instrument suits the times we live in.

One of the most striking things about the research for this book was finding that the distribution of recorder playing and the interest in composing for it is now so great. Wherever enquiries were pursued, enthusiastic players and composers were found. Even recorder players themselves are not generally fully aware of the current extent of the revival and tend to be taken aback to find that others are equally concerned with the future well-being of the instrument. In this sense, recorder playing is a sub-culture where there are as yet few internal channels of communication and little meaningful intercourse with the wider world of music.

What then is the appeal of the recorder? Apart from the obvious advantage that it is not unduly difficult to play, at least in the early stages, a more important quality for many is that it is a very 'personal' instrument. Not only are recorders small and portable, there is also a very direct physical relationship between the player's breath and the sound, with no 'hardware' intervening in the shape of reeds, complicated key-work, etc. Berio's description of the recorder as a 'human' instrument is an acute one. It is indeed one of the simplest and most natural-sounding of instruments, closest of all, perhaps, to that musical ideal, the human voice.

THE RECORDER IN AMATEUR AND EDUCATIONAL MUSIC

The recorder has always had a very strong amateur following, not only nowadays but in the seventeenth and eighteenth centuries also, as the

116

accounts of Pepys, Hawkins, Burney and others have demonstrated. Opportunities to play at amateur level are ever-increasing. Many countries have active recorder societies which run classes, ensemble groups and residential recorder courses and encourage domestic music-making. Another outlet for amateurs is the recorder orchestra, a comparatively new phenomenon which involves organising a large group of recorders, perhaps forty to fifty people, playing the full range of instruments from sopranino to contrabass in appropriately-balanced sections, rehearsing and functioning as an orchestra and playing works specifically composed or arranged for such a group. This concept in recorder playing was first explored by Rudolf Barthel in Germany in the 1950s. He arranged his players in a group of high-pitched and a group of low-pitched instruments, doubled at the octave, according to the principles set out by Mersenne in his *Harmonie Universelle* of 1636–7. This idea was further developed in Britain in the 1970s and 1980s by giving each instrumental group an independent line, as in any orchestra. Instead of playing consort music with as many as ten or more players to a part in music that was intended to be played one to a part, the recorder orchestra uses the instruments like the registers of the organ and the number of players to a part is arranged so as to give a balanced sound that is very attractive and different. The other important aspect of the recorder orchestra is that, because the music has been specially composed, it brings out the best features of each instrumental group and the imposition of orchestral discipline on amateur players is beneficial both to their playing and to their general musicianship.

The educational aspect of the recorder is also important. Fortunately the standard of recorder teaching is everywhere improving and where previously whole classes of pupils might have been taught almost by rote, thus acquiring very little real skill or interest in the instrument, now one is much more likely to find that tuition is available on the same basis and with the same status as that for other instruments. This has meant an increasing respect for the recorder and its music which has led in turn to a steady improvement in playing standards at all ages. Students can opt to progress through graded examination systems which no longer make any musical or technical concessions. Some, of course, pursue their studies at third level in music colleges and conservatoires where recorder is now quite widely, though not routinely, taught.

REPERTOIRE

Why does the recorder have so much more modern music than any of the other 'early' instruments? There are, of course, new works for harpsichord, lute, viol, etc. but the numbers are small by comparison with those for the recorder. The explanation that these instruments have nothing to offer in contemporary music seems improbable. For the answer, therefore, it appears that we must return to the question of supply and demand. Harpsichordists, lutenists, viol players and other 'early' musicians have a significantly greater amount of high-quality renaissance and baroque music at their disposal than have recorder players, and far more opportunities to play with chamber ensembles and orchestras, quite apart from the solo repertoire. As a result, the demand for new works to supplement recital programmes has not arisen to anything like the same extent. The early recorder repertoire, on the other hand, is small. For the soloist it centres on the baroque sonatas with basso continuo written in a period of just seventy years between 1680 and 1750 and some sonatas and canzonas from the early seventeenth century. For the ensemble player the repertoire of sixteenth- and seventeenth-century mixed consorts is somewhat bigger but still lacking in variety and real musical stimulus. The recorder player has therefore been forced actively to seek new areas of music-making.

A large body of recorder music has been accumulating over some fifty years now, yet it is noticeable that it contains very few works by first-rank composers. By comparison, a quick glance at the twentieth-century harpsichord repertoire will show that although it is smaller in quantity it contains such names as Busoni, Poulenc, Falla, Krenek, Orff, Martinû, Milhaud, Frank Martin, Cage, Xenakis, Ligeti, Carter and Babbitt. Why were these composers prepared to write for harpsichord and not for recorder? The revival of the two instruments, after all, progressed more or less in parallel.

The answer may perhaps lie at least partly in the fact that composers who felt themselves to be on secure ground when writing for an instrument like the harpsichord could well find themselves at a loss with the recorder. Even nowadays information about the instrument and what it can do is by no means easy to come by.

COMPOSITIONS OF STATURE

In assessing the quality of the modern recorder repertoire it must be said that the number of pieces that have established themselves permanently as compositions of real musical stature are few, perhaps ten per cent or less of the whole, but this is in fact a satisfactory percentage as a measure of quality in any art form. Among the top ten per cent, most players would put Berio's *Gesti*, Shinohara's *Fragmente*, Ishii's *Black Intention* and Hirose's *Meditation* as well as some earlier compositions such as the Berkeley *Sonatina*. The consort music of Cooke and Staeps is firmly established, especially among amateur players, and also Serocki's works; in particular, his *Arrangements* for one to four recorder players is very highly regarded. *Lamentation* by Hirose, *Periferisch-Diagonaal-Concentrisch* and *Installaties* by Geysen and *Les Moutons de Panurge* (1969) by Rzewski are fine examples of consort pieces, the last three based on repetitive compositional techniques.

118

Some of the newer additions to the consort repertoire are very good also. Examples are Malcolm Tattersall's *Alien Landscape II* (1982); Chiel Meijering's *Een Paard met Vijf Poten*; *Chasing...* (1985) by Benjamin Thorn; and *So Tear* by Willem Wander van Nieuwkerk. In the solo repertoire, Jan Rokus van Rosendael's *Rotations* (1988) has recently made a strong impact. Nowadays, performances of the more extreme improvisatory works such as Bussotti's *RARA* and *Rezitative* by Vetter are rare, as are performances of the conventional sonatas of the 1940s and 1950s.

The most developed section of the repertoire, as we have seen, is that of solo recorder or recorder with keyboard accompaniment. The recorder consort category, which had been somewhat neglected, is now expanding due to the influence of the Amsterdam Loeki Stardust Quartet (p. 124), who, as well as composing and arranging works themselves, have also provided the impetus for other composers. The combination of recorders with other instruments and/or voices is another category that should be capable of considerable further growth. It is important for the survival of the instrument that it should avoid being pushed into a ghetto, heard only in all-recorder programmes given before audiences composed almost exclusively of recorder enthusiasts, as happens very often at the moment. The availability of more good modern music using recorders in combination with other instruments would help to make it possible to bring the recorder to a wider public. It is only necessary to think of the cantatas of Handel and Bach, many of which use the recorder, as well as the concertos of Vivaldi, Sammartini, Telemann, etc. to realise that similar instrumental combinations should offer some interesting possibilities to contemporary composers. *Scènes Fugitives* (1961) by Rudolf Kelterborn and *Consort Music I* (1976) by Herman Rechberger are promising examples of the genre. One hopes that players will realise the importance of continuing to commission and perform new music from the best composers they can find.

THE RECORDER NOW

The direction which the recorder has taken in the twentieth century has been, to a great extent, dictated by the changing trends in musical thinking. Of those players who first brought the recorder into full prominence in contemporary music in the 1960s few are still actively involved with the instrument to the same extent. While Carl Dolmetsch continues tirelessly to promote the instrument, Frans Brüggen, on the other hand, is developing a successful conducting career with The Orchestra of the Eighteenth Century, which he founded in 1981. This leaves him increasingly little time for the recorder, although he still gives solo performances and tours with Walter van Hauwe and Kees Boeke as the 'Sour Cream' ensemble. Hans-Martin Linde also works with an authentic instruments ensemble, The Linde Consort, and con-

10 Sour Cream. From left: Walter van Hauwe, Frans Brüggen, Kees Boeke. This Dutch group, formed in the early 1970s, did much to update the 'safe' image of the recorder through the originality and wit of their performances.

11   Walter van Hauwe

tinues to teach at the Schola Cantorum Basiliensis. His recorder performances and composition have also diminished as other activities have taken
precedence. Michael Vetter continues to use recorder in his blending of music
and Buddhist meditation techniques but is now rather outside the
mainstream of recorder playing.

The Netherlands remains the mecca for all aspiring young professionals,
and is the place where the methodology of recorder teaching was formulated
by the successive teacher–pupil generations of Kees Otten, Frans Brüggen and
the present leading teachers, Walter van Hauwe and Kees Boeke. Students at
this level are nowadays better equipped technically than those of ten
or fifteen years ago and their ambition and professionalism are impressive.
Very often they play other instruments to a high standard too but still want
to make their careers with the recorder. The opportunities are scarce, however. Without the possibility of orchestral employment the prospects are
limited to professional performance as a soloist or in an ensemble, or to teaching. This seems to be the position in general everywhere at the present time.
To take but one example, in Britain the energies of leading players like Alan

Davis, Evelyn Nallen and Ross Winters tend to be taken up more with teaching than performance.

SETTLING DOWN

After two decades of experimentation during the 1960s and 1970s, some of it quite radical, recorder players and recorder music are beginning to show signs of settling down. The recorder music of the 1980s is less extreme in its effect and more mature in musical content. The desire to be outrageous, an important motivating force in the 1960s, has waned now that it has been amply demonstrated that the recorder does have a legitimate place in twentieth-century music. Works such as Andriessen's *Sweet*, du Bois's *Muziek* and Berio's *Gesti* are now central to the whole recorder repertoire and the study of extended techniques has become a necessary part of the training of every conservatoire student. We see, in fact, that while striving to get away from the restrictions of the past we have, as is inevitable in the evolution of any art form, been building a new set of traditions. As a consequence of this, the major innovation of our time, the development of extended techniques, can now be regarded as fully integrated into recorder playing, at least in professional circles.

The first indication of this gradual integration of extended techniques into recorder music can be seen in some of the compositions of the mid-1970s where, rather than being the whole *raison d'être* of the work, the techniques grow organically and very naturally out of the musical concept. Some fine examples of this are seen in the music of the Japanese composer Ryohei Hirose (b. 1930), in particular his *Meditation* for alto recorder solo and *Lamentation* for four recorders, both written in 1975. Both works are strongly influenced by the characteristic sounds and forms of Japanese traditional music and Hirose transfers many of the techniques native to the shakuhachi (end-blown bamboo notched flute) to the recorder. These include rustle tones, microtonal glissandos and various forms of vibrato (see pp. 100–4).

In *Lamentation*, the composer's aim was to create the effect of an ink-painting. This he does through the juxtaposition of continuous versus discrete sounds, light versus shade. The ever-changing forms and aspects of grief are conveyed with great intensity and expressiveness. The piece is very much homophonic in its intent; that is, all four instruments are treated as a single sound-producing unit with a common goal even when they are actually moving in polyphony. As in *Meditation*, the use of extended techniques is integral to the work. Microtonal glissandos are a particular feature, the shifting pitches conveying the search for emotional resolution. Other recent works show similar signs of the 'normalisation' of extended techniques.

Conclusions

Flautando (1981) for recorder trio and '*sich fragend nach frühster Erinnerung*' (1985) for recorder quartet by the Swiss composer Hans Ulrich Lehmann (b. 1937) are works with a strong compositional concept where modern techniques extend the range of sounds available without in any way dominating the texture.

There is now evidence of a growing trend away from extended techniques altogether. Many of the best compositions of the 1980s are entirely free of them, perhaps as a reaction to their excessive use in the past. One of the new styles to find a place in recorder music is that of minimalism. This uses small, tightly-controlled melodic units in continuous rhythmic repetition. The static harmonic effect thus created focusses the listener's attention on the fine detail as the patterns evolve. The origins of minimalism are to be found in the music of John Cage, La Monte Young and Terry Riley in the mid-1960s and their ideas have since been developed further by Philip Glass and Steve Reich. One of the first manifestations of minimalism in the recorder repertoire was to be seen in *Periferisch-Diagonaal-Concentrisch* (1972) for recorder quartet by the Belgian composer Frans Geysen (b. 1936). This was later followed by the same composer's *Installaties* (1983), also for recorder quartet, a representation in sound of the ceramic 'installations' of the artist Piet Stockmans. In both of these works Geysen uses a gradual metamorphosis of musical material which brings to the fore the sound qualities and attack characteristics of the recorders. Neither uses extended techniques although the performers are given the option of adding flutter-tonguing, vibrato, etc. at will in *Installaties*. Further successful examples of minimalism in recorder music are afforded by Willem Wander van Nieuwkerk's *So Tear* (1987) for three recorders and Chiel Meijering's *Een Paard met Vijf Poten* ('A Horse with Five Legs'; 1982, rev. 1984) for four recorders. These are humorous pieces and the Nieuwkerk also contains elements of rock music and jazz.

Works borrowed from the repertoire of other instruments have also broadened the perspectives of recorder players recently. These range from recorder performances of Varèse's *Density 21–5* (1936) and Terry Riley's seminal work *In C* (1964) to Mauricio Kagel's electro-acoustic music theatre piece *Atem* (1970) and an authorised transcription of Stockhausen's *In Freundschaft* (1977–84). Successful recorder transcriptions have also been made of works by Bartók, Stravinsky and Cage. The Estonian composer Arvo Pärt (b. 1935) has himself transcribed his pieces *Pari Intervallo* (1976), originally for organ, and *Arbos* (1977–86), originally for brass ensemble and percussion. Pärt's compositional style, blending elements of minimalism with plainsong and the chants of the Orthodox Church, draws a very beautiful sonority from the recorders. Some performers have even turned to the music of Machaut and other medieval masters, reinterpreting them in the light of twentieth-century idioms.

NEW GROUND

A number of players are breaking new ground in composition and performance, particularly in the Netherlands, which seems to be the source of most
new ideas at the moment. Among these may be mentioned Laurens Tan
(b. 1953) who has made a speciality of solo performance on the bass recorder,
exploring its rich sonorities and harmonics in his own very attractive and
unusual compositions using minimalist techniques. In Amsterdam, Walter
van Hauwe is extending his repertoire of solo recital music into both earlier
and later periods. A compact disc issued in 1988 contains, among other
things, thirteenth-century Japanese and fourteenth-century Italian music,
Varèse's *Density 21–5* and Debussy's *Syrinx*, both originally for flute, and
Stravinsky's *Pièces* nos. 1 and 2, originally written for clarinet. Kees Boeke
has addressed the problem of the small scale and brevity of much recorder
music. His own solo composition, *The Circle*, involves a metamorphosis of
musical material in a controlled improvisation through the circle of keys. It
lasts approximately forty minutes and uses no extended techniques. His performance of this work is compelling and he hopes to follow it up with further
large-scale compositions where the musical content takes precedence and the
recorder is used as a 'normal' instrument. One hopes that other composers
will follow his lead.

Outside the Netherlands new ideas are also appearing. The Canadian
player Peter Hannan specialises in electro-acoustic music using recorder and
hopes to extend his composing and playing to involve other instruments also.
Matthias Weilenmann of Zurich is inspired by the subtleties of expression in
recorder sound and is searching for new works in which a deeper musical content can be expressed without entering what he sees as the distorted region of
extended techniques.

The four recorder players of the Amsterdam Loeki Stardust Quartet,
Daniël Brüggen, Bertho Driever, Paul Leenhouts and Karel van Steenhoven,
have redefined the whole meaning of the recorder consort. They were first
launched upon an unsuspecting world when they became prizewinners at the
1981 Musica Antiqua Competition in Bruges. There they raised more than a
few eyebrows when they played Leenhouts's jazzy Stevie Wonder arrangement labelled *Report upon 'When shall the Sun shine?'* in the finals, a cheeky
departure from the expected serious repertoire. Since then, their success has
grown steadily with an increasing number of concerts in Europe, America
and the Far East and two recordings on the Decca L'Oiseau Lyre label, both
of which have received the prestigious Edison award.

Two problems face any chamber music group when it starts out: the choice
of a repertoire appropriate to the group and instruments appropriate to the
repertoire. Neither is easy to find and the Loeki Stardust Quartet have
expended much time and effort in choosing pieces that suit them and

12 The Amsterdam Loeki Stardust Quartet. From left: Bertho Driever, Paul Leenhouts, Daniël Brüggen, Karel van Steenhoven

recorders to match. Their concerts may range from Palestrina and Frescobaldi to Gibbons, Purcell, Bach and twentieth-century masterpieces such as Hirose's *Lamentation*. A particular hallmark is their judicious plundering of music from unexpected sources. One example of this is Bertho Driever's quartet arrangement of Vivaldi's *Concerto per Flautino*, RV 443, but they also play jazz by Charlie Parker and 'fun' pieces such as a hilarious arrangement by Paul Leenhouts of Henry Mancini's *Pink Panther* theme.

In October 1988 the first International Week for Twentieth-Century Recorder Music was held in Amsterdam, organised by Walter van Hauwe and a group of associates. Here for the first time was a major gathering of all those interested in modern recorder music. In an intensive week of concerts, master-classes and lectures the whole development of recorder music was placed under review. Composers, players and teachers from many parts of the world made contacts and exchanged opinions on what was good, what was bad, what was passé and who had the latest, most exciting ideas. Instead of being a complacent, back-slapping exercise it turned out to be a week of expectant optimism. Due respect was accorded to the achievements of earlier decades but all attention was focussed on the now and the hereafter. Most striking and encouraging was the high calibre of the participants, few of whom were over thirty-five years of age and all of whom were convinced that in the recorder lay their own personal musical expression and that, given the number of composers now involved with the instrument, all the ingredients were present for a bright future.

Appendix: Non-standard fingerings

FINGERING CHARTS

The following tables of non-standard fingerings for alto recorder have been selected from *Die Blockflöte in der zeitgenössischen Musik* (1987) by Herman Rechberger and reproduced by kind permission of the author.

Dynamic Variations

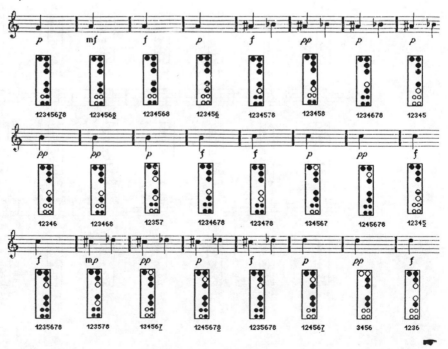

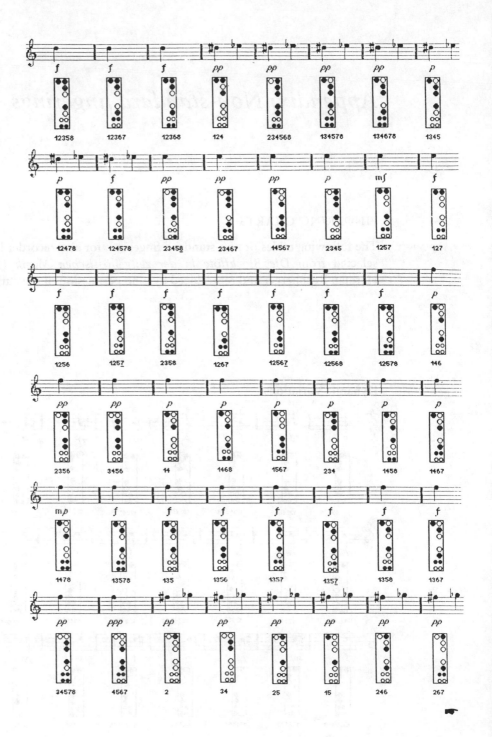

Timbre Variations

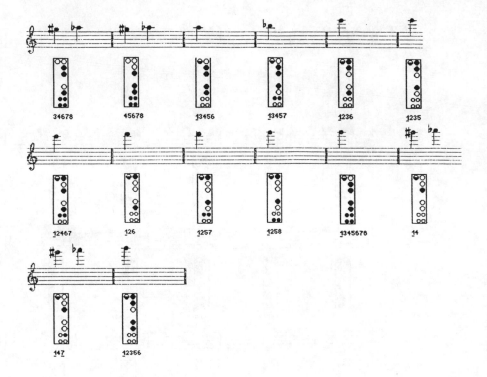

Non-standard fingerings

Harmonics (Open Register)

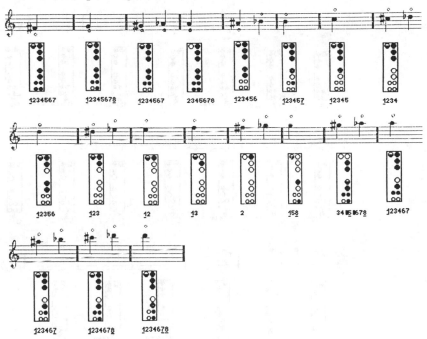

Appendix

Harmonics (Closed Register)

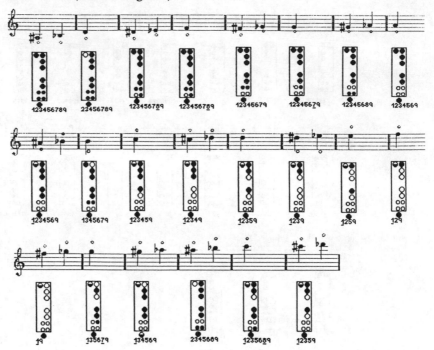

134

Non-standard fingerings

Harmonics (Covered Register)

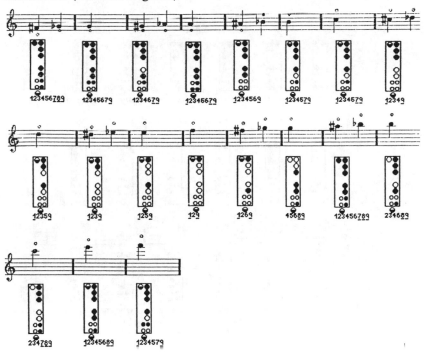

Appendix

Microtones

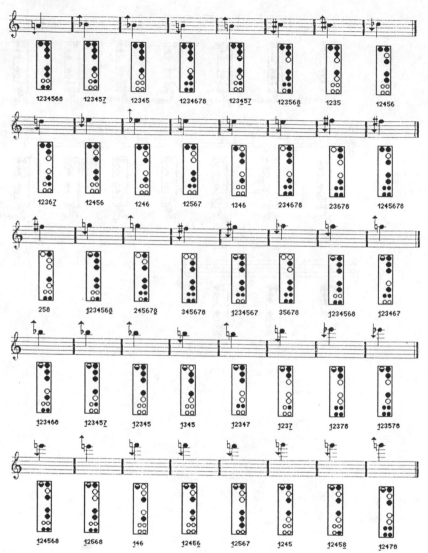

PART II SELECT CATALOGUE OF TWENTIETH-CENTURY RECORDER MUSIC

Introduction

The initial intention in compiling this catalogue was to produce a comprehensive listing of twentieth-century music for recorder. As research proceeded, however, it became apparent that the sheer volume of works was such as to make this impossible – indeed, in many respects unhelpful – within the present context. This select catalogue was therefore compiled with the aim of providing a realistic guide to the best of modern recorder music currently available. While every endeavour was made to be as objective as possible it must, inevitably, remain a somewhat personal selection.

The catalogue was compiled from scores obtained from music publishing houses and Music Information Centres all over the world. Research in library holdings, in music journals and in many works of reference yielded further compositions and, in addition, composers, performers and colleagues were helpful in bringing works to my attention. The following criteria governed the selection of works. First, only original compositions suitable for professional or semi-professional concert performance were included; pedagogical material and arrangements were excluded. Secondly, only works currently available from a commercial publisher or a public body such as a national music information centre were listed. Thirdly, only works which were felt to be of sufficient musical merit were selected. The total listing contains some 400 works out of about 800 known to me. There are inevitably exceptions to every rule, however, and I found myself unable to pursue these criteria with complete rigour. There are, therefore, occasional instances where an arrangement was included because its imagination or inventiveness made it unthinkable to exclude it; where a piece that is officially pedagogical was included because of its musical merit; and where, also because of its musical merit, an unpublished composition was listed although it is as yet only available in manuscript from the composer direct.

HOW TO USE THE CATALOGUE

Works are listed by category of instrumentation, with each entry giving the following standard information: composer's name and date of birth; title of the work; date of composition; publisher; instrumentation. Where a date of composition was not available the date of publication is given in parentheses following the name of the publisher. Occasionally dates of birth were withheld or were unavailable. Titles of compositions are given as on the title-page of the music. Sub-titles are added only when they significantly clarify the nature of the work. Names given in parentheses after the title, in the case of a vocal work, indicate the author of the text or, in the case of an arrangement, the composer of the original music.

Information on the instrumentation of each work is as detailed as possible. Where an alternative instrumentation is possible this is shown by an oblique stroke, e.g. 'a, hpd/pf', and the work is entered under the first, major category, in this case 'Recorder(s) and harpsichord or other keyboard instrument', and cross-referenced under the alternative instrumentation, 'Recorder(s) and piano'. Ambiguities arising from the use of alternative instrumentation are clarified by the use of parentheses: e.g. '(a, str qt)/(fl, pf)' means alto recorder and string quartet *or* flute and piano. If the instrumentation allows for an optional instrument, e.g. 'sno, s, a, t, b, gui *ad lib*', the work is entered under the category dictated by the full instrumentation, i.e. 'Recorder(s) and guitar', and cross-referenced under '5 or more recorders'. 'Sno, a, b (one player)' or 's, a, t, b (4 players)' etc. indicates that the performer(s) change instruments during the course of the work. The category 'Recorder(s) and voice(s)' contains only works using solo voices as part of a group of, at most, six performers. Larger ensembles using solo voices or chorus are categorised with 'Mixed instrumental ensembles: six or more performers'. The assignment of works to specific categories occasionally presented problems and in these cases the work was entered under the most obvious category with cross-references as necessary.

Abbreviations

RECORDERS

a	alto (treble)
b	bass
gt b	great bass
rec, recs	recorder, recorders
s	soprano (descant)
sno	sopranino
t	tenor

OTHER ABBREVIATIONS

arr.	arranged
b cl	bass clarinet
bn	bassoon
ch orch	chamber orchestra
cl	clarinet
elec db	electric double bass
elec gui	electric guitar
fl	flute
gui	guitar
hpd	harpsichord
incl.	including
inst	instrument(s)
MS	unpublished composition in manuscript only
ob	oboe
opt.	optional
orch	orchestra
org	organ
perc	percussion
pf	piano

140

Select catalogue of twentieth-century recorder music

str	strings
str orch	string orchestra
str qt	string quartet
trbn	trombone
va	viola
vc	violoncello
vn	violin
ww	woodwind
xyl	xylophone

Catalogue

SOLO RECORDER

Andriessen, Louis 1939–
1 Sweet, 1964. Schott   a
2 Ende, 1981. Ascolta   2a (one player)

Baer, Walter 1928–
3 Desolatio Marsyae, 1975. SMA   3 rec (one player)

Bandt, Ros 1951–
4 Meditation, 1976. AMC   a/fl/shakuhachi

Bank, Jacques 1943–
5 Blue Mosque, 1974. Donemus   bass rec player possessing baritone voice

Baur, Jürg 1918–
6 Mutazioni, 1962. Introduction and realisation by   a
   M. Vetter. Breitkopf & Härtel
7 Pezzi Uccelli, 1964. Breitkopf & Härtel   solo rec

Berio, Luciano 1925–
8 Gesti, 1966. Universal   a

Bozay, Attila 1939–
9 Solo, op. 30/a, 1978. MS   recs (one player)

Braun, Gerhard 1932–
10 Acht kleine Stücke, 1968. Hänssler   s
11 Monologe I, 1968–70. Hänssler   recs (one player)
12 Minimal Music II, 1971–2. Moeck   sno, s, a, t, b (one or several players)
13 Rezitative und Arien, 1975. Moeck   t
14 Inmitten der Nacht, 1977. Moeck   s
15 Monologe II, 1980. Hänssler   b
16 Schattenbilder, 1980. Moeck   a

142

Bresgen, César 1913–88

17 Nachruf für eine Amsel, 1974. Moeck   recs in C and F (one
                                                  player)

Bussotti, Sylvano 1931–

18 RARA, 1966. Graphic score with introduction and   solo rec
    realisation by M. Vetter, Ricordi

Cooke, Arnold 1906–

19 Serial Theme and Variations, 1966. Schott   a
20 Inventionen. Moeck (1980)   a

Dolci, Amico 1957–

21 Nuovi Ricercari 1–3. Heinrichshofen (1974)   a
22 Nuovo Ricercare 5, 1973. Heinrichshofen   a

Du Bois, Rob 1934–

23 Muziek, 1961. Schott   a
24 Pastorale VII, 1964. Moeck   a
25 Spellbound, 1976. Donemus   contrabass rec in F

Eisma, Will 1929–

26 Hot, powdery stones, 1968. Donemus   a

Gasser, Ulrich 1950–

27 Seeland, 1982. Ricordi   a
28 Schtei, 1985–6. Moeck   t

Gieseler, Walter 1919–

29 Breviarium, 1960. Moeck   a/fl

Hashagen, Klaus 1924–

30 Gardinenpredigt eines Blockflötenspielers, 1969.   s, a, t, b (one player)
    Hänssler

Heider, Werner 1930–

31 Katalog, 1965. Ed. M. Vetter. Moeck   sno, a, b (one player)

Hekster, Walter 1937–

32 Encounter, 1973. Donemus   solo rec

Hirose, Ryohei 1930–

33 Meditation, 1975. Zen-On   a

Ishii, Maki 1936–

34 Black Intention, 1975. Zen-On   s, s (low pitch), t,
                                                      tam-tam (one player
                                                      only)

Kölz, Ernst 1929–

35 Gesang der Sirenen. Doblinger (1978)   a

Kröll, Georg 1934–

36 Con Licenza, 1971. Moeck   a

Lechner, Konrad 1911–89

37 Traum und Tag, 1975. Moeck   s
38 Spuren im Sand, 1976. Moeck   solo rec in C
39 Varianti, 1976. Moeck   t
40 Vom andern Stern, 1987. Moeck   s

Linde, Hans-Martin 1930–

41 Fantasien und Scherzi, 1963. Schott   a
42 Four Caprices, 1966. Heinrichshofen   a
43 Music for a Bird, 1968. Schott   a
44 Amarilli mia bella, 1971. Schott   s, a, b (one player)
45 Märchen, 1977. Schott   s, a, t, b (one player)
46 Inventionen. Noetzel (1959)   solo rec
47 Blockflöte virtuos, 1983. Schott   a

McCabe, John 1939–

48 Desert IV: Vista, 1983. In 'A Birthday Album for   sno, t (one player)
Thomas Pitfield'. Forsyth

Man, Roderik de 1941–

49 Séance, 1986. Donemus   a/fl

Marti, Heinz 1934–

50 Ombra, 1979. Hug   b (or other low ww inst)

Masumoto, Kikuko 1937–

51 Pastorale, 1973. Zen-On   s, t (one player)

Matuszčzak, Bernadetta 1937–

52 Improvvisazione und Associazione antiche, 1982.   s/t
Moeck

Miller, Edward J. 1930–

53 Song. McGinnis & Marx (1964)   s/a

Moser, Roland 1943–

54 Alrune, 1979. Hug   a

Nicholls, David 1955–

55 Theatre Piece 4: In the Cage (T. Hodges), 1986.   sop, s, a (one player),
MS   opt. wind-chimes and
     metronomes

Nobis, Herbert 1941–

56 Sieben Phasen, 1977. Moeck   a

O'Leary, Jane 1946–

57 Two for One, 1986. IMIC   a, voice flute (one player)

Poulteau, Pierre 1927–

58 Sonatine. Leduc (1980)   a

Rechberger, Herman 1947–

59 Comme l'on s'amuse bien (G. Apollinaire), 1978.   a, bells, metronomes,
    Edition Modern   wind chimes, mouth
    organ (one player)

60 Il Fa-To-Re, 1978. Edition Modern   a
61 *pp*, 1982. FMIC   t (prepared)

Riehm, Rolf 1937–
62 Gebräuchliches, 1972. Moeck   a

Roosendael, Jan Rokus van 1960–
63 Rotations, 1988. Donemus   a

Shinohara, Makoto 1931–
64 Fragmente, 1968. Schott   t

Staeps, Hans Ulrich 1909–88
65 Virtuose Suite, 1961. Schott   a

Stockhausen, Karlheinz 1928–
66 In Freundschaft, 1977–84. Stockhausen-Verlag   a

Tattersall, Malcolm 1952–
67 Franklin River, 1980. Cootamundra Music   a
68 Ikaho, 1981. Cootamundra Music   b

Thommessen, Olav A. 1946–
69 The Blockbird, 1981. Lyonn   a/t

Thorn, Benjamin 1961–
70 The Voice of the Crocodile . . . , 1988. AMC   b

Veilhan, Jean-Claude 1940–
71 Les Nations en Folies, 1981. Leduc   sno, s, a (one player)
72 Liens, 1971. Leduc   a

Vetter, Michael 1943–
73 Figurationen III, 1966. Moeck   solo rec

See also Catalogue nos. 172, 187, 420

TWO RECORDERS

Badings, Henk 1907–87
74 Suite no. 3, 1958. Harmonia Uitgave   2s

Bank, Jacques 1943–
75 The memoirs of a cyclist, 1967, rev. 1970. Donemus   2a

Berkeley, Lennox 1903–89
76 Allegro, 1955. Boosey & Hawkes   2a

Bresgen, César 1913–88
77 Sieben Stücke, 1981. Moeck   a, t

Cooke, Arnold 1906–
78 Six duets, 1976. Moeck   2s (or other inst of equal pitch)

Dolci, Amico 1957–
79 Nuovo Ricercare 4. Heinrichshofen (1975)   2a

Gál, Hans 1890–1987
80 Six Two-Part Inventions, op 68b, 1957. Doblinger   s, a

Genzmer, Harald 1909–
81 Tanzstücke, 2 vols. Schott (1973)   2a

Gümbel, Martin 1923–86
82 Drei kleine Studien. In 'Duettspielbuch für   2s
Sopranblockflöten'. Hänssler (1965)

Hirose, Ryohei 1930–
83 Ode I, 1979. Zen-On   b/a, b/t
84 Ode II, 1980. Zen-On   2a

Hoogwegt, Trees 1957–
85 Tekanemos, 1979. Moeck   s, a, t (two players)

Linde, Hans-Martin 1930–
86 Elegia und Rondo. In 'Duettspielbuch für   2a
Altblockflöten'. Hänssler (1965)
87 Scherzi und Notturni. In 'Duettspielbuch für   2s
Sopranblockflöten'. Hänssler (1965)

Łuciuk, Juliusz 1927–
88 Monologi i dialogi, 1977. PWM   2s

Martinů, Bohuslav 1890–1959
89 Divertimento, 1957. Eschig   2s/2a

Migot, Georges 1891–1976
90 Suite in 3 movements, 1957. Bärenreiter   s, a

Nobis, Herbert 1941–
91 Per Due, 1980. Moeck   2a

Staeps, Hans Ulrich 1909–88
92 Reihe kleiner Duette. Schott (1950)   2a

Stockmeier, Wolfgang 1931–
93 Konversation, 1977. Moeck   2a

Thorn, Benjamin 1961–
94 5s and 6s and 7s, 1987. AMC   s/t, a/b

Tippett, Michael 1905–
95 Four Inventions. Schott (1954)   s, a

Waxman, Donald 1925–
96 Duo Sonatine. Galaxy (1972)   2a

146

Weiss, Arleta 1959–
97   Pan-epikon, 1982. Moeck   2s

See also Catalogue nos. 12, 172, 187, 188, 343, 402

THREE RECORDERS

Angerer, Paul 1928–
98   Musica trifida. Doblinger (1983)   2a, t

Badings, Henk 1907–87
99   Trio, 1955. Moeck   2s, a
100 Suite no. 2. Harmonia Uitgave (1957)   3s

Bornefeld, Helmut 1906–
101 Concentus, 1980. Moeck   sno, s, a, t, b (3 players)

Britten, Benjamin 1913–76
102 Alpine Suite, 1955. Boosey & Hawkes   2s, a

Buschmann, Rainer Glen 1929–
103 New Moods for Flutes, 1979. Moeck   2s, a

Cooke, Arnold 1906–
104 Sonatina, 1972. Moeck   s, a, t
105 Pieces for three, 1981. Moeck   s, a, t

Fricker, Peter Racine 1920–90
106 Suite. Schott (1956)   2a, t

Gál, Hans 1890–1987
107 Divertimento, op. 98. Schott (1972)   s, a, t

Genzmer, Harald 1909–87
108 Trio, 1942. Schott   s, 2a

Gümbel, Martin 1923–86
109 Flötenstories. Moeck (1976)   3 rec of equal pitch

Hamburg, Jeff 1956–
110 Passacaglia, 1983. Donemus   3b (amplified)

Heider, Werner 1930–
111 La Leggenda di Sant'Orsola, 1981. Moeck   3t

Hindemith, Paul 1895–1963
112 Trio (from the 'Plöner Musiktag'), 1932. Schott   s, a, a/t

Kiyose, Yasuji 1900–
113 Trio for recorders, 1972. Zen-On   a, t, b

Lehmann, Hans Ulrich 1937–
114 Flautando, 1981. Edition Gravis   a, t, a/t (3 players)

Linde, Hans-Martin 1930–
115 Trio für Blockflöten, 1966. Hänssler   sno, a, t, b (3 players)

Miller, Edward J. 1930–

116 3 Trios, 1958. McGinnis & Marx   a, t, b (3 players)

Müller-Hartmann, Robert 1884–1950

117 Suite. Schott (1951)   s, a, t

Nieuwkerk, Willem Wander van 1955–

118 So Tear, 1978. Ascolta   3 rec

Staeps, Hans Ulrich 1909–88

119 Saratoga Suite, 1965. Galaxy   s, a, t
120 Trio, 1972. Doblinger   2a, t

Stiebler, Ernstalbrecht 1934–

121 Obligat, 1974. Edition Modern   a, t, b

Stockmeier, Wolfgang 1931–

122 3 Episoden: Musik mit Volksliedern, 1972. Moeck   3a

Thorn, Benjamin 1961–

123 Chasing . . . , 1985. AMC   a, t, b

See also Catalogue nos. 12, 172, 187, 188, 282, 327, 353, 355

FOUR RECORDERS

Badings, Henk 1907–87

124 Quartett I. Harmonia Uitgave (1980)   s, a, t, b
125 Quartett II. Harmonia Uitgave (1979)   s, a, t, b
126 Quartett III, 1978. Harmonia Uitgave   s, a, t, b
127 Quartett IV. Harmonia Uitgave (1979)   s, a, t, b
129 Quartett V. Harmonia Uitgave (1980)   s, a, t, b
129 Quartett VI. Schulz (1981)   s, a, t, b
130 Quartett VII. Harmonia Uitgave (1983)   s, a, t, b

Baines, Francis 1917–

131 Quartet. Schott (1960)   2a, 2t

Baur, Jürg 1918–

132 Tre per Quattro, 1972. Breitkopf & Härtel   s, a, t, b

Bechtcl, Helmut 1929–

133 Quartett für Blockflöten. Moeck (1976)   s, a, t, b

Britten, Benjamin 1913–76

134 Scherzo, 1955. Boosey & Hawkes   s, a, t, b

Buschmann, Rainer Glen 1929–

135 Moods for Flutes. Moeck (1963)   2s, a, t

Charlton, Andrew 1928–

136 Idyllwild Suite, 1964. Berandol   s, a, t, b
137 Three Movements for Four Recorders. Galaxy (1970)   s, a, t, b

Clemencic, René 1928–
138   Chronos II, 1975. Moeck   s, a, t, b

Cooke, Arnold 1906–
139   Suite. Moeck (1966)   s, a, t, b
140   Quartett für Blockflöten, 1970. Moeck   s, a, t, b
141   Suite no. II, 1983. Moeck   s, a, t, b

Davis, Alan 1947–
142   Party Pieces. Schott (1987)   s, a, t, b

Doppelbauer, Josef Friedrich 1918–
143   Zehn Stücke, 1977. Doblinger   s, a, t, b

Eitan, Zohar 1955–
144   The Twittering Machine, 1977, rev. 1980. IMI   s, a, t, b

Gál, Hans 1890–1987
145   Quartettino, op. 78, 1960. Universal   2s, a/t, t/b

Genzmer, Harald 1909–
146   Quartettino. Schott (1958)   s, a, t, b

Geysen, Frans 1936–
147   Periferisch-Diagonaal-Concentrisch, 1972. Schott   s, a, t, b (4 players)
148   Installaties, 1983. Moeck   s, a, t, b (4 players)

Graves, John
149   Suite. Schott (1974)   2s, a, t

Hand, Colin 1929–
150   Fenland Suite. Schott (1973)   s, 2a, t

Hirose, Ryohei 1930–
151   Lamentation, 1975. Zen-On   2a, t, b
152   Idyll I, 1976. Zen-On   s, a, t, b (4 players)

Huber, Nicolaus A. 1939–
153   Epigenesis I, 1967–8. Bärenreiter   recs (4 players)

Joubert, John 1927–
154   Dr. Syntax, op. 85. Nova (1981)   (s, a, t, b)/(s, 2a, 2t, 2b)

Kiyose, Yasuji 1900–
155   Recorder Quartet, 1969. Zen-On   s, a, t, b

Krol, Bernhard 1920–
156   Prova per Quattro in tre argumenti, op. 63/2.   2a, t, b
      Bärenreiter (1982)

Leenhouts, Paul 1957–
157   Report upon 'When shall the sun shine?', 1981.   s, a, t, b
      Moeck
158   On the Trail of the Pink Panther (after Mancini),   a, t, b, gt b
      1987. Moeck

Lehmann, Hans Ulrich 1927–
159 'sich fragend nach frühster Erinnerung', 1985.   2t, 2b
      Edition Gravis

Manneke, Daniël 1939–
160 Ordre, 1976. Donemus   sno, a, t, b

Meijering, Chiel 1954–
161 Een Paard met Vijf Poten, 1982, rev. 1984.   s, a, t, b (4 players)
      Donemus

Meilink, Stef 1950–
162 Polyphonics, 1980. Donemus   s, a, t, b

Mondrup, Christian 1947–
163 Kleines Quartett, 1970. Moeck   s, a, t, b

Pärt, Arvo 1935–
164 Pari Intervallo, 1976. Universal   s, a, t, b

Poser, Hans 1917–70
165 Rendsburger Tänze, op. 42, 1957. Sikorski   s, a, t, b

Rubbra, Edmund 1901–86
166 Air and Variations, op. 70. Lengnick (1957)   s, a, t, b
167 Notturno, op. 106. Lengnick (1962)   s, a, t, b

Ruiter, Wim de 1943–
168 Blockfluitkwartet, 1977. Donemus   s, a, t, b

Saux, Gaston 1885–1969
169 Quartet in F. Schott (1961)   s, a, t, b
170 Quartet no. 2 in G. Schott (1965)   s, a, t, b

Serocki, Kazimierz 1922–81
171 Improvisations. Moeck (1960)   s, a, t, b
172 Arrangements for one to four recorders, 1975–6.   s, a, t, b (4 players)
      PWM/Moeck

Staeps, Hans Ulrich 1909–88
173 Sieben Flötentänze. Doblinger (1954)   s, 2a, t
174 Dort nied'n in jenem Holze, 1958. Doblinger   s, a, t, b
175 Partita in C, 1963. Moeck   s, a, t, b

Steenhoven, Karel van 1958–
176 Wolken, 1984. Moeck   4a

Stockmeier, Wolfgang 1931–
177 3 Episoden: Strukturen und Refrain, 1973. Moeck   s, 3a

Vaughan Williams, Ralph 1872–1958
178 Suite for Recorders, 1939. OUP   s, a, t, b

Whitney, Maurice C. 1909–58
179 The Bass Quartet. Loux Music (1985)   4b

Witzenmann, Wolfgang 1937–
180 Bordun. Moeck (1976)   s, a, t, b
181 Bordun II, 1977. Moeck   s, a, t, b
182 Bordun III, 1982. Moeck   s, a, t, b

See also Catalogue nos. 12, 187, 188

FIVE OR MORE RECORDERS

Baines, Francis 1917–
183 Fantasia. Schott (1956)   3s, 3a

Harvey, Raymond 1922–
184 Suite no. I, 1959, rev. 1969. Nova   s, a, 2t, b

Linde, Hans-Martin 1930–
185 Browning. Moeck (1988)   s, a, t, b (5 players)

Marez Oyens, Tera de 1932–
186 Relaxations, 1971. Donemus   s, a, t, b (more than one
                                                               to a part)

Moser, Roland 1943–
187 Musik zu Pontormo, 1986. SMA   1 to 8 recs

Rzewski, Frederic 1938–
188 Les Moutons de Panurge, 1969. Zen-On   any no. of recs or other
                                                               inst *ad lib.*

Staeps, Hans Ulrich 1909–88
189 Rondelli, 1962. Moeck   2s, 2a, t
190 Chorisches Quintett, 1963. Universal   s, 2a, t, b
191 Arkadische Szene, 1978. Doblinger   s, a, 2t, b
192 Des Einhorns Anmut, 1978. Doblinger   s, a, t, b (more than one
                                                               to a part)
193 Berliner Sonate, for 3-part octave-doubling rec   s+t, s+t, a+b
    ensemble, 1979. Universal

Tattersall, Malcolm 1952–
194 Alien Landscape II, 1982. Cootamundra Music   2a, 2t, b

Taylor, Stanley 1902–72
195 Capriol Suite (after Warlock), 1926. Boosey &   s, 2a, t, b/t
    Hawkes

Urbanner, Erich 1936–
196 Nachtstück, 1978. Doblinger   a, 2t, 2b, gt b

See also Catalogue nos. 12, 154, 378, 383

Select catalogue of twentieth-century recorder music

RECORDER(S) AND PIANO

One recorder

Andriessen, Louis 1939–
197 Paintings, 1965. Graphic score with introduction   rec/fl, pf
by M. Vetter. Moeck
198 Melodie, 1976. Schott   a, pf

Arnold, Malcolm 1921–
199 Sonatina, op. 41, 1953. Paterson   a, pf

Ball, Michael 1938–
200 Danserye, op. 21, 1983. Forsyth   s, pf

Bank, Jacques 1943–
201 Two, 1979. Donemus   b/cl, pf

Baur, Jürg 1918–
202 Incontri, 1960. Breitkopf & Härtel   a, pf

Bergmann, Walter 1902–88
203 Sonata, 1965. Schott   s, pf
204 Sonata, 1973. Schott   a, pf

Berkeley, Lennox 1903–89
205 Sonatina, op. 13, 1940. Schott   a, pf

Bornefeld, Helmut 1906–
206 Sonatine, 1978. Hänssler   s, pf

Braun, Gerhard 1932–
207 Nachtstücke, 1972. Moeck   sno, s, a, t, b (one player), pf

Bush, Alan 1900–
208 Duo Sonatina, op. 82. Nova (1981)   s, a, t, (one player), pf

Casken, John 1949–
209 Thymehaze. Schott (1979)   a, pf

Du Bois, Rob 1934–
210 Spiel und Zwischenspiel, 1962. Donemus   a, pf
211 Adagio Cantabile, 1979. Donemus   t, pf

Eisma, Will 1929–
212 Wonderen zijn schaars, 1965. Moeck   a, pf

Febel, Reinhard 1952–
213 Sechs Bagatellen, 1978. Moeck   a, pf

Frantz, Michel
214 Fleurs animées, Billaudot (1985)   sno, s, a, t (one player), pf

Genzmer, Harald 1909–
215   Sonata 1, 1941. Schott   a, pf
216   Sonata 2. Schott (1973)   a, pf

Giefer, Willy 1930–
217   Cadenza, 1970. Gerig   a, pf

Graves, John
218   Divertimento. Schott (1964)   a, pf

Hand, Colin 1929–
219   Sonata Breve, 1971. Schott   a, pf

Hovland, Egil 1924–
220   Cantus II, 1974–5. Norsk Musikforlag   s, pf

Jacob, Gordon 1895–1984
221   Sonata. Musica Rara (1967)   a, pf

Jacobi, Wolfgang 1894–1972
222   Fünf Studien, 1956. Moeck   a, pf

Jacques, Michael 1944–
223   Midsummer Suite, Roberton (1979)   a/fl, pf

Kelkel, Manfred 1929–
224   Sonatine, op. 9. Moeck (1970)   s, pf

Lechner, Konrad 1911–89
225   Ludus Juvenalis I, 1938, rev. 1975, Moeck   a, pf
226   Metamorphosen. Hänssler (1967)   s, a, (one player), pf/hpd

Leigh, Walter 1905–42
227   Sonatina, 1939. Schott   a, pf

Linde, Hans-Martin 1930–
228   Sonata in D minor, 1961. Schott   a, pf
229   Musica Notturna, 1968. Hänssler   a, pf/hpd
230   Fünf Studien, 1974. Schott   a, pf

Matz, Arnold 1904–
231   Sonata Contrappuntistica, 1970. Zen-On   a, pf

Medek, Tilo 1940–
232   Ikebana, 1975–6. Moeck   a, pf

Milford, Robin 1903–59
233   Sonatina in F. OUP (1958)   a, pf

Nobis, Herbert 1941–
234   Miniaturen, 1970. In 'Neuzeitliches Spielbuch für   a, pf
      Altblockflöte und Klavier'. Schott

Poole, Geoffrey 1949–
235   Skally Skarecrow's Whistling Book, 1978. Forsyth   a, pf

Poser, Hans 1917–70

236	Sonatina 1, op. 36/1. Sikorski (1957)	s, pf
237	Sonatina 2, op. 36/2. Sikorski (1956)	a, pf
238	Sonatina 3, op. 36/3. Sikorski (1956)	t, pf
239	Sieben Bagatellen, op. 52. Moeck (1963)	a, pf

Reizenstein, Franz 1911–68

240	Partita, op. 13, 1938. Schott	a, pf

Rubbra, Edmund 1901–86

241	Passacaglia sopra 'Plusieurs Regrets', op. 113. Lengnick (1964)	a, pf

Schilling, Hans Ludwig 1927–

242	Suite, 1954. Moeck	s, pf

Schollum, Robert 1913–

243	Sonatine, 1966. Doblinger	a, pf

Sollima, Eliodoro 1926–

244	Sonata. Schott (1973)	a, pf
245	Evolutioni no. 3. Heinrichshofen (1978)	a, pf

Staeps, Hans Ulrich 1909–88

246	Sonata in E flat major, 1951. Universal	a, pf
247	Sonata in C minor 'In modo Preclassico'. Galaxy (1967)	a, pf
248	Fantasia con Echo. Doblinger (1974)	s/t, pf

Stockmeier, Wolfgang 1931–

249	Sonatine, 1963. Schott	a, pf

Turner, John 1943–

250	Four Diversions, 1968–9. Forsyth	s, pf
251	Six Bagatelles, 1979–83. Forsyth	s, pf

Wilson, James 1922–

252	Duo, op. 85, 1982. IMIC	a, pf/hpd

See also Catalogue nos. 258, 259, 268, 269, 273, 278, 287, 289, 304, 392

Two or more recorders

Genzmer, Harald 1909–

253	Sonate. Schott (1956)	2a, pf

Staeps, Hans Ulrich 1909–88

254	The Newspaper Concerto for singing recorder players, 1966. Moeck	2s, a, pf
255	Vier Arietten, 1968. Doblinger	s, a, pf

See also Catalogue nos. 282, 283, 388

Select catalogue of twentieth-century recorder music

RECORDER(S) AND HARPSICHORD OR OTHER KEYBOARD
INSTRUMENT

One recorder

	Badings, Henk 1907–87	
256	Sonata, 1957. Donemus	a, hpd
	Bank, Jacques 1943–	
257	Song of Sitting Bull, 1973. Donemus	alto rec player possessing baritone voice, org
	Bornefeld, Helmut 1906–	
258	Florilegium, 1977. Universal	sop, s, a, t, b (one player), org/pf
	Borris, Siegfried 1906–87	
259	Sonata, op. 65, no. 1. Heinrischshofen (1975)	a, hpd/pf
	Broadstock, Brenton 1952–	
260	Aureole 3, 1984. AMC	a, hpd
	Butterley, Nigel 1935–	
261	The White-Throated Warbler, 1965. Albert	sno, hpd
	Doorn, Frans van 1930–	
262	Sonate, 1983. Donemus	s, hpd
	Dorward, David 1933–	
263	Concert-Duo. Heinrichshofen (1977)	s, hpd
	Eisma, Will 1929–	
264	Affairs II, 1963. Donemus	s, a (one player), hpd
	Flothius, Marius 1914–	
265	Cantilena e Ritmi, op. 48/2, 1961. Donemus	a, hpd
	Gál, Hans 1890–1987	
266	Drei Intermezzi. Schott (1974)	a, hpd
	Gümbel, Martin 1923–86	
267	Interludien, 1964. Hänssler	a, hpd
	Jacob, Gordon 1895–1984	
268	Variations. Musica Rara (1967)	a, hpd/pf
269	Sonatina, 1985. Studio Music Co.	a, hpd/pf
	Linde, Hans-Martin 1930–	
270	Sonatine Française, 1963. Hänssler	s, hpd
	Manneke, Daniël 1939–	
271	Clairobscur, 1978. Donemus	a, org
	Mellnäs, Arne 1933–	
272	The Mummy and the Humming-Bird, 1974. STIM	sno, s, a (one player), hpd

155

	Murrill, Herbert 1909–52	
273	Sonata, 1950. OUP	a, hpd/pf
	Rubbra, Edmund 1901–86	
274	Meditationi sopra 'Coeurs Désolés', op. 67, 1949. Lengnick	a, hpd
275	Sonatina, op. 128, 1964. Lengnick	a, hpd
	Schollum, Robert 1913–	
276	Sonata, op. 76, 1968. Doblinger	a, hpd
	Staeps, Hans Ulrich 1909–88	
277	Dialogue, 1958. Hänssler	a, hpd
	Stockmeier, Wolfgang 1931–	
278	Duo mit Suiten-Fragmenten, 1982. Moeck	a, hpd/pf/org
	Toebosch, Louis 1916–	
279	Ommimeloog, op. 104, 1972. Donemus	s, hpd
280	Bilingua, op. 112, 1977. Donemus	s, org/hpd
	Walter, Heinz 1928–	
281	Partita Impulsiva, 1967. Doblinger	s, hpd

See also Catalogue nos. 226, 229, 252, 289

Two or more recorders

	Cooke, Arnold 1906–	
282	Suite, 1972. Moeck	s, a, t, opt. hpd/pf
	Eder, Helmut 1916–	
283	Melismen, op. 58/2. Doblinger (1974)	s, a, hpd/pf
	Thorn, Benjamin 1961–	
284	Much Cuckoo, 1980. AMC	4s, 4a, org

RECORDER(S) AND GUITAR

	Berkeley, Michael 1948–	
285	Pas de Deux, 1985. OUP	rec, gui
	Buschmann, Rainer Glen 1929–	
286	Very New Moods, 1984. Moeck	s, a, gui
	Duarte, John W. 1919–	
287	Three Simple Songs without Words, op. 41. Broekmans & van Poppel (1971)	a/s, gui/pf
	Gál, Hans 1890–1987	
288	Divertimento, op. 68c, 1957. Doblinger	2a, gui

Golland, John 1942–

289 New World Dances, op. 62, 1980. Forsyth   s, a, (one player),
                                                   gui/hpd/pf

Griffiths, John 1952–

290 Conversation Piece, 1976. Zimmerman   a, gui

Hoddinott, Alun 1929–

291 Italian Suite, op. 92, 1977. OUP   a, gui

Hollfelder, Waldram 1924–

292 Episoden, 1982. Moeck   s, gui

Kröll, Georg 1934–

293 Canzonabile. Moeck (1976)   a, t, b (one player), gui

Linde, Hans-Martin 1930–

294 Musica da Camera. Schott (1974)   rec, gui
295 Music for Two, 1983. Schott   a, gui

Smith Brindle, Reginald 1917–

296 Hathor at Philae, 1982. Schott   a, gui

Stockmeier, Wolfgang 1931–

297 Divertimento, 1968. Moeck   2a, gui

Wessmann, Harri 1949–

298 Suite, 1979. FMIC   a, gui

RECORDER(S) AND STRINGS

Bozay, Attila 1939–

299 Improvisations no. 2, op. 27, 1976. Editio Musica   recs (one player), str trio

Dolci, Amico 1957–

300 Nuovo Ricercare 6, 1974. Heinrichshofen   sno, s, a (one player), vn,
                                                   vc

Gál, Hans 1890–1987

301 Suite, op. 68, 1956. Doblinger   s/t, vn
302 Trio Serenade, op. 88, 1966. Schauer   a/fl, vn, vc

Heppener, Robert 1925–

303 Arcadische Sonatine, 1959. Donemus   2a, vn

Jacob, Gordon 1895–1984

304 Suite, 1957. OUP   (a, str qt)/(a, pf)

Korda, Victor 1900–

305 Vier Stücke. Doblinger (1976)   a, vn

Kox, Hans 1930–

306 Cyclophonie IV, 1965. Donemus   a, 6 vn, 2 vc, db

Marez Oyens, Tera de 1932–

307 3 Modi, 1973. Donemus   s, a, t, b, 3 vn, vc

Poser, Hans 1917–70
308 Acht Duette. Möseler (1970) a, vn

Stockmeier, Wolfgang 1931–
309 3 Episoden: Hör-Spiel, 1974. Moeck 5a, vn

Straesser, Joep 1934–
310 Duplum, 1977. Donemus b, vc (amplified)

RECORDER(S) AND VOICE(S) (EXCLUDING CHORUS)

Alwyn, William 1905–85
311 Seascapes (M. Armstrong). Forsyth (1985) soprano voice, a, pf

Ball, Michael 1938–
312 To Musick, 1983. In 'A Birthday Album for soprano and counter-
Thomas Pitfield'. Forsyth tenor voices, a, pf

Beckwith, John 1927–
313 Les Premiers Hivernements, 1986. CMC soprano, tenor voices,
2 rec, lute, viol, perc

Bedford, David 1937–
314 The Juniper Tree (T. Bagg), 1982. Universal soprano voice, sno, s
(one player), hpd

Braun, Gerhard 1932–
315 Gärten der Nacht (R. Frier), 1983. Moeck soprano voice, s, a, t, b
(one player), pf

Crosse, Gordon 1937–
316 A Wake Again, 1986. OUP (hire only) 2 countertenors, 2 rec,
vc, hpd
317 Verses in Memoriam David Munrow, 1979. OUP countertenor, rec, vc,
(hire only) hpd

Dickinson, Peter 1934–
318 A Memory of David Munrow, 1977. Novello 2 countertenors, 2 rec,
viola da gamba, hpd

Du Bois, Rob 1934–
319 Songs of Innocence (W. J. Wegerif), 1974. Donemus countertenor, t, db

Gunn, Douglas 1935–
320 O Men from the Fields (P. Colum), 1973. IMIC soprano voice, t, vc, hpd

Guy, Barry 1947–
321 Waita, 1980. Novello (hire only) tenor voice, rec

Joubert, John 1927–
322 The Hour Hand, op. 101 (E. Lowbury), 1984. soprano voice, a
Novello

Leeuw, Ton de 1926–
323 4 Liederen, 1955. Donemus medium voice, s, a, t

Leighton, Kenneth 1929–88

324 Animal Heaven, op. 83 (W. Whitman, J. Dickey), 1980. Novello — soprano voice, rec, vc, hpd

Nieuwkerk, Willem Wander van 1955–

325 Blokken, 1988. Ascolta — mezzo-soprano voice, rec, 2 perc, tape

Rubbra, Edmund 1901–86

326 Cantata Pastorale, op. 92. Lengnick (1962) — high voice, a, vc, hpd

Staeps, Hans Ulrich 1909–88

327 Das Lied tönt fort, 1963. Doblinger — (s, a, t)/(str), voices *ad lib.*

328 Amnis aevi omnipotens, 1966. Doblinger — medium voice, rec in C, pf

See also Catalogue nos. 5, 332, 370, 372, 373, 400

MIXED INSTRUMENTAL ENSEMBLES

Two to five performers

Angerer, Paul 1928–

329 Quartett I, 1971. Doblinger — a, viola da gamba, gui, perc

Bank, Jacques 1943–

330 Die Ouwe, 1975. Donemus — b, b cl, pf
331 Wave, 1975. Donemus — b, 2 perc

Bedford, David 1937–

332 Because he liked to be at home (K. Patchen), 1974. Universal — treble rec player possessing tenor voice, harp

Berkeley, Lennox 1903–89

333 Concertino, op. 49, 1955. Chester — s/fl, vn, vc, hpd/pf

Berkeley, Michael 1948–

334 American Suite, 1980. OUP — rec/fl, bn/vc

Bornefeld, Helmut 1906–

335 Arkadische Suite, 1930. Hänssler — a, one bell

Braun, Gerhard 1932–

336 Acht Spielstücke, 1974. Moeck — s, perc
337 Fünf Miniaturen, 1969. Bosse — s, pf, 2 perc
338 Triptychon, 1983. Moeck — a, t, b (one player), 2 perc

Dickinson, Peter 1934–

339 Translations, 1971. Novello — rec, viola da gamba, hpd

Du Bois, Rob 1934–
340 Pastorale II, 1963–9. Donemus   a, fl, gui

Eliscu, Robert 1944–
341 Träne I and II, 1974. Edition Modern   Metallophone, rec, 2 xyl

Furrer-Münch, Franz 1924–
342 Details IV, 1975. Edition Modern   recs (one player), vc/viola da gamba, org

Gasser, Ulrich 1950–
343 Thurland, 1982. SMA   a, fl/2a

Gentilucci, Armando 1939–
344 Diario II, 1971. Ricordi   rec, ob, cl

Heider, Werner 1930–
345 Musik im Diskant, 1970. Hänssler   sno, hpd, perc
346 Gassenhauer, 1984. Moeck   s/piccolo, perc

Hirose, Ryohei 1930–
347 Potaraka, 1972. Zen-On   a, vc, hpd

Hollinger, Roland
348 Sept Pièces-Séquences. Billaudot (1987)   s, a, t, b (one player), perc

Holmboe, Vagn 1909–
349 Trio, op. 133. Hansen (1981)   rec, vc, hpd

Hovland, Egil 1924–
350 Cantus VI, op. 118, 1982. Norsk Musikforlag   rec, fl, pf

Joubert, John 1927–
351 Sonata à Cinque, op. 43, 1963. Novello   a, 2 vn, vc, hpd

Ketting, Piet 1904–84
352 Fantasia, 1969. Donemus   s, a (one player), fl, hpd

Kiezer, Henk 1948–
353 Rondo, 1981, rev. 1985. Donemus   s, a, t, perc (3 players, amplified)

Lechner, Konrad 1911–89
354 Engramme, 1982–3. Moeck   sno, a, t, b (one player), hpd, perc
355 Lumen in Tenebris, 1980. Moeck   s, a, t, b, perc (3 players)

Linde, Hans-Martin 1930–
356 Trio, 1960. Schott   a, fl, hpd
357 Divertimento, 1964. Moeck   a, perc
358 Serenata à tre. Schott (1966)   s/t/b, gui, vc
359 Consort Music, 1972. SMA   recs, crumhorns, str, perc (4 players)

McIntosh, Diana

360 User-friendly, 1987. CMC   s, db

Mathias, William 1934–

361 Concertino, op. 65, 1974. OUP   a/fl, ob, bn, hpd/pf

Rechberger, Herman 1947–

362 Dolce ma non troppo!, 1979–80. FMIC rec, perc

Roxburgh, Edwin 1937–

363 Constellations, 1983. MS   s, ob

Rubbra, Edmund 1901–86

364 Fantasia on a Theme of Machaut, op. 86, 1957. a, str qt, hpd
  Lengnick

365 Fantasia on a chord, op. 154, 1977. Lengnick rec, hpd, viola da gamba
                    ad lib.

Segerstam, Leif 1944–

366 Episode no. 2, 1978. FMIC   a, fl, gui

Terzakis, Dimitri 1938–

367 Omega 2, 1983. Edition Gravis   t, perc

Toebosch, Louis 1916–

368 Mayetmâr, op. 99, 1968. Donemus a, fl, hpd
369 Muziek, op. 116, 1980. Donemus s, viola da gamba, hpd

Six or more performers

Bank, Jacques 1943–

370 Put me on my bike no. 1, 1971. Donemus baritone voice, a, mixed
                 choir (16 voices)

Clemencic, René 1928–

371 Maraviglia III, 1968. Universal   sno, a, b (3 or more
                 players), str (3 or more
                 players), trbn, perc

372 Sesostris I, 1970. AMIC   rec, hpd, viola da gamba,
                 gui, perc, child's voice
                 (taped)

Eliscu, Robert 1944–

373 The Man of Madras, 1974. Edition Modern voice, org, rec,
                 rauschpfeifen, perc, gui,
                 double bass

Furrer-Münch, Franz 1924–

374 A la Fenêtre d'en Face, 1976. SMA b, female voices

Henze, Hans Werner 1926–

375 Spielmusiken (from the opera *Pollicino*). Schott amateur orch incl. 3 sno,
  (1981)   3s, 2a, t, b

Hirose, Ryohei 1930–

376 Karavinka, 1973. Zen-On   rec, ob, str, perc

Kagel, Mauricio 1931–

377 Musik für Renaissanceinstrumente, 1965–6.   23 inst incl. recs
Universal

Konietzny, Heinrich 1910–

378 Scherzo-vice-versa, 1968. Bosse   sno, s, a, t, 2b, triangle,
ad lib.

Linde, Hans-Martin 1930–

379 Capriccio, 1963. Schott   s, a, t, 3 violas da gamba,
hand drum

Manneke, Daniël 1939–

380 Motet for renaissance instruments, 1975. Donemus 2s, 2a, 2t, b and other
inst

Meijering, Chiel 1954–

381 Hot summernights in autumn, 1978. Donemus   8 sno, 4a, 4t, 4b, ob, hpd,
(all rec parts doubling
sno)

Nasveld, Robert 1955–

382 Antifoon, 1977. Donemus   amateur choir and orch
(incl. 80–100
recs)

Pärt, Arvo 1935–

383 Arbos, 1977–86. Universal   s, a, t, b (7 or 8 players),
3 triangles *ad lib.*

Regt, Hendrik de 1950–

384 Musica, op. 10, 1971. Donemus   s, 2 vn, va, vc, hpd

Rimmer, John 1939–

385 The Exotic Circle, 1974. Kiwi Music   sno, s, a, t, b, gt b, 2 perc

Serocki, Kazimierz 1922–81

386 Impromptu Fantasque, 1973. PWM/Moeck   sno, s, a, t, b, gt b,
3 mandolins, 3 gui, perc,
pf

Staeps, Hans Ulrich 1909–88

387 Aubade und Tanz, 1957. Doblinger   s, a, t, b (6 players), gui,
pf

388 Tänze auf dem Lande, 1962. Doblinger   2s, a (more than one to a
part), pf, perc *ad lib.*

See also Catalogue no. 424

Select catalogue of twentieth-century recorder music

RECORDER CONCERTOS

Bank, Jacques 1943–
389 Recorders, 1981. Donemus   sno, s, a, t, b (one player), str, perc

Baur, Jürg 1918–
390 Concerto da Camera, 1975. Breitkopf & Härtel   rec, ch orch

Charlton, Andrew 1928–
391 Concerto da Camera, 1964. Berandol   a, str orch

Cooke, Arnold 1906–
392 Concerto, 1957. Schott (piano reduction available)   a, str orch

Kelterborn, Rudolf 1931–
393 Scènes Fugitives, 1961. Bärenreiter (hire only)   a, orch

Linde, Hans-Martin 1930–
394 Konzert, 1969. Schott   sno, a, b (one player), str orch

Rechberger, Herman 1947–
395 Consort Music 1, 1976. Jasemusiikki Ky   s, a (one player), ch orch
396 Consort Music 2, 1977. Jasemusiikki Ky   2 renaissance-music instrumentalists (rec, other inst), orch

Ridout, Alan 1934–
397 Chamber Concerto, 1979, MS   a, str orch, perc

Segerstam, Leif 1944–
398 Capriccio, 1967. Fazer   sno, orch

Serocki, Kazimierz 1922–81
399 Concerto alla cadenza, 1974. PWM/Moeck   sno, s, a, t, b, gt b (one player), orch

RECORDER(S) AND ELECTRONICS

Bank, Jacques 1943–
400 Blind Boy Fuller no. 1, 1966, rev. 1968. Donemus   a, pf, voice, tape
401 Maraens trompetten, 1980. Donemus   2a (amplified), tape

Dickinson, Peter 1934–
402 Recorder Music, 1973. Novello   (rec, tape)/(2 rec)

Dubrovay, László 1943–
403 Sequence. Editio Musica (1977)   rec, synthesiser

Eliscu, Robert 1944–
404 Aus der Vogelperspektive, 1979. Edition Modern   ob, rec, bamboo flute, tree trunks, tape

Gümbel, Martin 1923–86

405 Notturno. Moeck (1977)   b, tape, 2 gongs (one
                                                              player only)

Hashagen, Klaus 1924–

406 Gesten, 1966. Ed. M. Vetter, Moeck   s, a, t, b (one player),
                                                              tape

407 Pan 2-mal. Zimmerman (1987)   s, a, t, b (two players)
                                                              live electronics

Karkoshka, Erhard 1923–

408 mit/gegen sich selbst, 1969. Hänssler   s, a, t, b (one player),
                                                              tape

409 Flöten-/Tonband-Spiele, 1978. Moeck   one or more recorder
                                                              players with one or more
                                                              tape recorders

Man, Roderik de 1941–

410 Entanglements, 1987. Donemus   sno, a, t, b (one player),
                                                              tape

Marturet, Eduardo 1956–

411 Canto Llano, 1978. MS   s/t, tape delay

Osborne, Nigel 1948–

412 Passers-By, 1976. Universal   b, vc, synthesiser

Prooijen, Anton van 1939–

413 XIIOOO MLS, 1974. Donemus   s, bn, perc, voice, choir,
                                                              typewriter, tape

Rechberger, Herman 1947–

414 Pre-Inter-Post-Ludium, 1975. FMIC   a, live electronics

Schat, Peter 1935–

415 Hypothema, op. 20, 1969. Donemus   t, tape

Schönbach, Dieter 1931–

416 Canzona da Sonar III, 1967. Ed. M. Vetter. Moeck   s, pf, tape

Stahmer, Klaus Hinrich 1941–

417 Odysseia (Homer), 1981. Edition Gravis   sno, s, a, t, b (3 players),
                                                              tape

Thorn, Benjamin 1961–

418 Newrotika, 1981. AMC   a/b, live electronics
419 Pipistrelli Gialli, 1985. AMC   b, live electronics

Tosi, Daniel 1953–

420 Astrid '002, 1984. Editions Salabert   sop, s, a, t, b (one
                                                              player), with or without
                                                              tape

Truax, Barry 1947–
421 East Wind, 1981. CMC

a, t (one player, amplified), tape

Vetter, Michael 1943–
422 Rezitative, 1967. Moeck

rec, live electronics

Wilby, Philip 1949–
423 Breakdance, 1988. Chester

s, a, t, b/gt b (one player), tape

Wolff, Christian 1934–
424 Electric Spring II, 1966–70. Peters

a, t (one player), elec gui, elec db, gui, trbn, bass trbn *ad lib.*

See also Catalogue nos. 110, 310, 325, 353, 372

Index to catalogue

Publishers and Music Information Centres

NOTE An asterisk denotes Music Information Centres, e.g. AMC, FMIC. In the Catalogue works followed by these designations are unpublished, but copies may be had by application to the appropriate Centre.

Albert	J. Albert & Son Pty. Ltd, New York
*AMC	Australian Music Centre, Sydney, Australia
*AMIC	Austrian Music Information Centre, Vienna
Ascolta	Ascolta Music Publishing, Houten, Netherlands
Bärenreiter	Bärenreiter Verlag, Kassel/Basel/London
Berandol	Berandol Music Ltd, Toronto
Billaudot	Gérard Billaudot, Paris
	Boosey & Hawkes Music Publishers Ltd, London
	G. Bosse Verlag, Regensburg, Federal Republic of Germany
Breitkopf & Härtel	Breitkopf & Härtel, Wiesbaden/London
Broekmans	Broekmans & van Poppel, Amsterdam
Chester	J. & W. Chester Ltd, London
*CMC	Canadian Music Centre, Toronto
Cootamundra Music	Cootamundra Music, West Brunswick, Victoria
Doblinger	Verlag Doblinger, Vienna/Munich
*Donemus	Stichting Donemus, Amsterdam
Edition Gravis	Edition Gravis, Bad Schwalbach, Federal Republic of Germany
Editio Musica	Editio Musica, Budapest
Edition Modern	Edition Modern, Munich
Editions Salabert	Editions Salabert, Paris
Eschig	Edition Max Eschig, Paris
Fazer	Oy Musiikki Fazer AB, Helsinki
*FMIC	Finnish Music Information Centre, Helsinki
Forsyth	Forsyth Bros. Ltd, Music Publishing Division, Manchester
Galaxy	Galaxy Music Corporation, New York
Gerig	Edition Gerig, Cologne
Hansen	Edition Wilhelm Hansen, Copenhagen
Hänssler	Hänssler Verlag, Stuttgart

Publishers and Music Information Centres

Harmonia Uitgave	Harmonia Uitgave, Hilversum, Netherlands
Heinrichshofen	Heinrichshofen Verlag, Wilhelmshaven, Federal Republic of Germany
Hofmeister	VEB Friedrich Hofmeister Verlag, Leipzig, German Democratic Republic
Hug	Hug & Co., Musikverlag, Zurich
*IMI	Israel Music Institute, Tel Aviv
*IMIC	Irish Music Information Centre, Dublin
Jasemusiikki Ky	Jasemusiikki Ky, Hämeenlinna, Finland
Kiwi Music	Kiwi Music, Wellington, New Zealand
Leduc	Editions Musicales Alfonse Leduc, Paris
Lengnick	Alfred Lengnick & Co. Ltd, South Croydon, Surrey
Loux Music	Loux Music Publishing Co., New York
McGinnis & Marx	McGinnis & Marx, New York
Moeck	Hermann Moeck Verlag, Federal Republic of Germany
Möseler	Möseler Verlag, Wolfenbüttel/Zurich
Musica Rara	Musica Rara, London
Noetzel	Otto Heinrich Noetzel Verlag, Wilhelmshaven, Federal Republic of Germany
Norsk Musikforlag	Norsk Musikforlag A/S, Oslo
Nova	Nova Music, London
Novello	Novello & Co. Ltd, Sevenoaks, Kent
OUP	Oxford University Press Music Dept, London
Paterson	Paterson's Publications Ltd, London
Peters	Peters Edition Ltd, London
PWM	Polskie Wydawnictwo Muzyczne, Krakow
Ricordi	G. Ricordi & Co. Ltd, Milan/London
Roberton	Roberton Publications, Aylesbury, Bucks
Schauer	Schauer & May Ltd, London
Schott	Schott & Co. Ltd, London/Mainz
Schulz	Edition Schulz, Freiburg im Breisgau, Federal Republic of Germany
Sikorski	Musikverlag Hans Sikorski, Hamburg
*SMA	Schweizerisches Musik-Archiv, Zurich
*STIM	Informationscentral föf Svensk Musik, Stockholm
Stockhausen Verlag	Stockhausen Verlag, Federal Republic of Germany
Studio Music Co.	Studio Music Co., London
Universal	Universal Edition, London/Vienna
Zen-On	Zen-On Music Co. Ltd, Toyko
Zimmermann	Musikverlag Wilhel, Zimmermann, Frankfurt-am-Main, Federal Republic of Germany

Bibliography

FURTHER READING

Very little has as yet been published about the recorder as a twentieth-century instrument. The main general work of reference on the recorder, Edgar Hunt's *The Recorder and its Music* (Hunt 1962, rev. 1977), is concerned mainly with the historical recorder but provides a valuable account of the revival, particularly in England, in which the author played a major part. Gerhard Braun's short handbook *Neue Klangwelt auf der Blockflöte* (Braun 1978) presents a brief account of the development of modern recorder music and playing techniques before proceeding to a discussion of eight contemporary compositions. The work is a useful introduction to the subject but leaves many areas uncovered.

There are several good handbooks dealing with recorder technique and interpretation in general (Linde 1974; Waitzman 1978; Wollitz 1982; Davis 1983; and van Hauwe 1984 and 1987), some of which contain material on twentieth-century music and extended techniques. The first such handbook to specialise in modern techniques for recorder was *Il Flauto Dolce ed Acerbo* (1969) by Michael Vetter. In this he gives ten tables of non-standard fingerings listing harmonics, standard pitches and multiphonics of the open, closed and covered registers as well as white noise of the closed and covered registers. Standard pitches and harmonics are fairly thoroughly investigated with as many as fifty or more alternatives given for some notes. The investigation of multiphonics is not quite so thorough and although a great many fingerings are listed, they are not always accurate and reliable. The fingering tables are accompanied by a set of technical exercises and a brief but useful discussion of recorder technique.

Herman Rechberger's more recent researches into the technical aspects of modern recorder music are given in his handbook *Die Blockflöte in der zeitgenössischen Musik* (1987). He has compiled a series of tables of non-standard fingerings for alto recorder and these list fingerings for standard pitches, harmonics and multiphonics in the open, closed and covered registers as well as further fingerings for dynamic variations, microtones, etc. in the open registers. A selection of these is reproduced here. Rechberger lists only those fingerings which he feels have proved their reliability and can, therefore, be recommended to composers and performers with some degree of confidence. His treatise is more concise and, for the novice, easier to use than Vetter's and also includes a section devoted to examples of the notation of modern recorder music.

Les Sons multiples aux flûtes à bec by Martine Kientzy (1982) deals exclusively with multiphonics and presents 'a selection of only 1191 fingerings from the 2170 classified during preliminary research work'. This very detailed compilation gives fingerings for multiphonics on sopranino, soprano, alto, tenor and bass recorders together with a description, under various headings, of the technical and musical qualities of each set of sounds. The Australian player Ian Shanahan is also now working on a classification and description of extended recorder techniques. The fruits of his researches so far are to be found in Shanahan 1985. For serious students, it is of interest to read treatises on extended techniques for other instruments, such as those quoted here in the bibliography.

Notation in contemporary recorder music is frequently unconventional, as is the case in twentieth-century music in general, and this area has been well covered in Ursula Schmidt's useful book *Notation der neuen Blockflötenmusik: ein Überblick* (Schmidt, 1981).

Alker's *Blockflöten-Bibliographie*, recently updated (1984), contains listings of recorder music currently in print as well as books and articles about the recorder. It is of limited use to the reader interested in serious contemporary composition, however, since works from all periods are listed but without dates of composition or any indication whether they are historical or modern. Pedagogical material is also included, again without any distinction between it and the concert repertoire.

Alker, H. 1984; first edition 1966. *Blockflöten-Bibliographie*. Vol. I: Systematisches Teil Neuausgabe. Vol. II: Alphabetisches Teil. Wilhelmshaven.

Arnell, R. 1967. Arnold Cooke: a birthday conversation. *Composer* 24: 18–20.

Baines, A. 1957. *Woodwind Instruments and their History*, London.

Bartolozzi, B. 1967. *New Sounds for Woodwind*, London.

Bate, P. 1979; first edition 1969. *The Flute*, London.

Benade, A. H. 1976. *Fundamentals of Musical Acoustics*, New York.

Bergmann, W. 1972. Further notes on Hindemith's Recorder Trio. *American Recorder* 13: 17.

Boeke, K. 1982. Recorder now. *Early Music* 10: 7–9.

Braun, G. 1978. *Neue Klangwelt auf der Blockflöte*, Wilhelmshaven.

Brüggen, F. 1966. Berio's 'Gesti'. *Recorder and Music* 2: 66.

Campbell, M. 1975. *Dolmetsch: the Man and his Work*, London.

Clark, P. 1971. Another view of the Michael Vetter concert. *Recorder and Music* 3: 338.

Davis, A. 1983. *Treble Recorder Technique*, London.

Dawney, M. 1972. Arnold Cooke. *Composer* 45: 5–9.

Dempster, S. 1979. *The Modern Trombone*, Berkeley, Ca.

Dick, R. 1975. *The Other Flute*, London.

Dolmetsch, C. 1960. An introduction to the recorder in modern British music. *The Consort* 17: 47–56.

1968. Which way to turn the clock? *Recorder and Music* 2: 283–4.

Bibliography

Driscoll, D. A. 1967. Acoustical characteristics of the alto recorder. *American Recorder* 8: 109–13.

Galpin, F. W. 1932. *Old English Instruments of Music* (third edition), London.

Ganassi, S. 1535. *Opera intitulata Fontegara*, Venice. Edited by H. Peter, translated by D. Swainson, Berlin Lichterfelde, 1959.

Haskell, H. 1988. *The Early Music Revival*. London

Hauwe, W. van. 1984, 1987. *The Modern Recorder Player*, 2 vols., London.

Haynes, B. 1968. The decline: a further scrutiny. *Recorder and Music* 2: 240–2.

Higbee, D. 1965. The etymology of 'recorder'. *Galpin Society Journal* 18: 128.

Hotteterre, J. le R. 1707. *Principles of the Flute, Recorder and Oboe*, translated by D. Lasocki, London, 1968.

Howell, T. 1974. *The Avant-Garde Flute*, Berkeley, Ca.

Hunt, E. 1962; revised 1977. *The Recorder and its Music*, London.

Kientzy, M. 1982. *Les Sons multiples aux flûtes à bec*, Paris.

Kottick, E. L. 1974. *Tone and Intonation on the Recorder*, New York.

Linde, H.-M. 1974. *The Recorder Player's Handbook*, London.

Marvin, B. 1972. Recorders and English flutes in European collections. *Galpin Society Journal* 25: 30–57.

Mersenne, M. 1636. *Harmonie Universelle*, Paris.

Moeck, H. 1978. Zur 'Nachgeschichte' und Renaissance der Blockflöte. *Tibia* 1 and 2.

Morgan, F. 1982. Making recorders based on historical models. *Early Music* 10: 14–21.

Musical Times 1885. Historical concerts at the Inventions Exhibition. Vol. 26: 477–9 (unsigned).

Nederveen, J. C. 1969. *Acoustical Properties of Woodwind Instruments*, Amsterdam.

Neumayer, D. 1976. Hindemith's Recorder Trio: sketches and autograph. *American Recorder* 17: 61–8.

Paap, W. 1970. Frans Brüggen and the recorder. *Sonorum Speculum*, Spring, 9–16.

Praetorius, M. 1618. *Syntagma Musicum: De Organographia*, vols. I and II, Wolfenbüttel. Translated and edited by D. Crookes, Oxford, 1986.

Rechberger, H. 1987. *Die Blockflöte in der zeitgenössischen Musik*. Finnish Music Information Centre, Helsinki.

Rehfeld, P. 1977. *New Directions for Clarinet*, Berkeley, Ca.

Reichenthal, G. 1980. A profile of Hans Ulrich Staeps. *American Recorder* 20: 144–8.

Schmidt, U. 1981. *Notation der neuen Blockflötenmusik: ein Überblick*, Celle, Federal Republic of Germany.

Shanahan, I. L. 1985. The avant-garde recorder: a preliminary study of some recent developments in alto recorder playing techniques and their notation. Unpublished dissertation (B.Mus.), University of Sydney.

Staeps, H. U. 1966. Saratoga Suite: a commentary. *American Recorder* 7: 5–6.

Tattersall, M. 1984. Australian music for recorder. *The Recorder* 1: 19–22, Melbourne.

1987. Wider horizons: more Australian recorder music. *The Recorder* 6: 5–8, Melbourne.

Thompson, J. M. 1972. *Recorder Profiles*, London.

Bibliography

Trowell, B. 1957. King Henry IV, recorder-player. *Galpin Society Journal* 10: 83–4.

Turetzky, B. 1974. *The Contemporary Contrabass*, Berkeley, Ca.

Vetter, M. 1967. New recorder music from Holland. *Sonorum Speculum*, Summer, 19–25.

1968. Apropos Blockflöte. *Melos* 35: 461–5.

1969. *Il Flauto Dolce ed Acerbo*, Celle, Federal Republic of Germany.

Waitzman, D. 1967. The decline of the recorder in the 18th century. *Recorder and Music* 2: 222–5.

1978. *The Art of Playing the Recorder*, New York.

Weber, R. 1976. Recorder finds from the Middle Ages and results of their reconstruction. *Galpin Society Journal* 29: 35–41.

Welch, C. 1911. *Six Lectures on the Recorder and other Flutes in Relation to Literature*, London.

Wollitz, K. 1982. *The Recorder Book*, London.

General index

References to illustrative material are italicised

acoustics, 27–8, 90
Adler recorders, 9
alto recorder, *see* recorder family
amateur recorder playing, *see* recorder playing
American Recorder Society, 18
amplification, *see* electro-acoustic music
Amsterdam Loeki Stardust Quartet, 101, 119, 124–5, *125*
Andriessen, Louis, 16, 51; *Ende*, 70, 114; *Paintings*, 59, 72; *Sweet*, 53, 54, 103, 122
archaeological evidence, 20
articulation (*see also* breathy flutter-tongue, flutter-tonguing and sputato tonguing), 26, 52, 60, 76, 83–4, *83*, 91–4, 99; double tonguing, 93; single tonguing, 91–2; triple tonguing, 93
Association Française pour la Flûte à Bec, 17
Aulos recorders, 19
Australia, 18–19
authenticity, *see* performance practice
avant-garde music, *see* repertoire
avant-garde techniques, *see* techniques, extended

Badings, Henk: *Sonata*, 44–5, 52
bamboo pipes, 8, 20
Bandt, Ros, 18
Bank, Jacques, 70; *Blind Boy Fuller no. 1*, 78; *Maraens Trompetten*, 63, 78; *Memoirs of a Cyclist*, 70–1; *Die Ouwe*, *109*, 109–10; *Put me on my bike no. 1*, 71, 72; *Recorders*, 63; *Two*, 63
Bärenreiter recorders, 9
Barker, Michael, 36, 79–81
Barthel, Rudolf, 117

Bartók, Béla: recorder transcriptions, 123
bass recorder, *see* recorder family
Bate, Stanley, 13, 38, 44
Baur, Jürg, 51–2; *Incontri*, 52; *Mutazioni*, 16, 52, 53, 90, 90–1; *Pezzi Uccelli*, 16, 52–3
Belgium, 1–2, 4–5
bell key, *see* recorder, mechanical devices
bent tones (*see also* glissando), 89
Bergmann, Walter, 42–3
Berio, Luciano, 52, 55, 64, 116; *Gesti*, 14, 53–7, *56*, 104–5, 118, 122
Berkeley, Lennox, 13; *Sonatina*, 38–9, 118
Berkeley, Michael, 13
Boeke, Kees, 62, 119, *120*, 121; *The Circle*, 124
bore, *see* recorder: design
Bozay, Attila, 18
Braun, Gerhard, 12, 18, 61; *Inmitten der Nacht*, *113*; *Minimal Music II*, 63, 93, 94, *105*, *111*, 114; *Monologe I*, 61–2, 63, 88, 114; *Nachtstücke*, 61–2, *109*; *Schattenbilder*, 61–3, *105*, *110*
breath pressure, 52, 55, 86, 88, 203–4, 112
breathing, 26, 55–6, 84; circular, 18, 106
breathy flutter-tongue, 99
breathy tones, *see* rustle tones
Bressan recorders, 5, 7, 31
Bridge, Joseph Cox, 5
Britten, Benjamin, *45*, 45–7; *Alpine Suite*, 45–6; *Noye's Fludde*, 45; *Scherzo*, 45
Brüggen, Frans, 12–14, *14*, 16, 50–1, 54–5, 57, 60, 62, 70, 79, 115, 119, *120*, 121
Bussotti, Sylvano, 73, 75; *La Passion selon Sade*, 73, 75; *RARA*, 16, 64, 72–5, *74*, 76, *111*, 119

175

General index

General index

General index

Netherlands (*cont.*)
music, 14, 16, 44–5, 50–3, 59–60, 63,
70–1, 79, 123; recorder revival, 11–12
New Zealand, 18
noise effects (*see also* mouth sounds, percussive effects *and* white noise), 99, 103,
106, 112–14
non-standard fingering, *see* fingering

open form, 37, 52, 57–8
Orff, carl, 11
Otten, Kees, 13, 44–5, 121
overblowing, 27–8, 55, 57–8, 69, 71, 93,
101, 103, 112

Paetzold, Herbert, 79, *80*
Pärt, Arvo: *Arbos*, 123; *Pari Intervallo*, 123
percussive effects (*see also* mouth-sounds),
61–2, 76–7, 104–6, 114
performance practice, 3, 9, 12–13, 32–3
performances, early recorder, 2, 4–5
performer, focus on, 66–70
Peter, Hildemarie, 7
Petri, Michala, 18, 62
pitch (*see also* recorder: range), 6, 10, 26–8,
31–4, 41–3, 67, 84, 89–90, 96, 101, 103
Poland, 18
Pope, Peter, 13, 38
Poser, Hans, 44
Prescott recorders, 19

quarter-tones, *see* microtones
random finger-play, 57–8, 61, 71, 103–4,
106
Rawsthorne, Alan, 38
Rechberger, Hermann, 18, 83, 85, 112;
Appendix, 127–35; *Comme l'on s'amuse
bien*, 66, 72; *Consort Music I*, 79, 99,
119; *Dolce ma non troppo!*, 72; *pp*, 112
recorder, 20–36, *21*; baroque, 7, 9, 22, 23,
30–2, 34–5; 'improved', 9, 31, 34;
modern, 11–19, 32–6, *33, 80*; renaissance, 23, 28–30, *29*, 23–5
recorder: decline of, 4, 31; derivation of
name, 20–1; description, 21–5, *21, 22*;
design, 9–10, 25–36, baroque, 30–1,
34–5, bore construction, 4, 9, 23, 28,
30–1, *33, 35*, innovations, 34–5, modern,
34–6, renaissance, 28–9, *29*, 35; mechanical devices, 34; musical characteristics,
25–6, 31; range (*see also* pitch), 24–5, 27,
32, 48, 115; revival, 1–19, 37–40, 43–4,
116; sound production in (*see also* acous-

tics), 21; structural alterations, 18, 53,
76, 111–14; two recorders, one player,
67–70, 114–15
recorder family, 8, 22, 23, 24–5, 29, 48, 90;
alto (treble), 7, 23, 35, 116; bass, 19, 23,
57, 90, 114, 124; contrabass, 23, 79–81,
80; garkleinflötlein, 115; great bass, 23;
sopranino, 23, 115; soprano (descant),
23, *33*, 35; tenor, 23, 57, 114
recorder makers, 5–10, 19, 31–2, 34–5, 43
recorder making, 4–11, 32–6; mass-
production, 7–10, 32, 35; material, 19,
26, 28, 35–6; rediscovery of, 5–6n, 7–10
recorder music, *see* repertoire
recorder orchestra, 117
recorder playing, 4, 11, 62–3, 116; amateur,
8, 11, 17–18, 45, 47, 116–17
register break, 98
registers, 84–8, 90, 133–5
Reizenstein, Franz: *Partita*, 38–9, 44
repertoire, 11–14, 17, 19, 37, 117–18,
122–5; avant-garde, 37, 50–63; baroque,
11, 118; conventional, 37–49; electro-
acoustic, 77–81; graphic, 72–7; renaissance, 118; of stature, 118–19; theatrical,
64–71
Ridout, Alan, 13
Riehm, Rolf: *Gebräuchliches*, 92
Riley, Terry, 123; *In C*, 123
Rimmer, John, 18
Roessler recorders, 19
Rokus van Rosendael, Jan: *Rotations*, 119
Rose, Pete, 18, 106
Rubbra, Edmund, 13, 46; *Fantasia on a
Theme of Machaut*, 46; *Meditazioni
sopra 'Coeurs Désolés'*, 38, 46; *Sonatina*,
38, 46
rustle tones, 51, 73, 99–100, 122
Rzewski, Frederic: *Les Moutons de
Panurge*, 118

Schat, Peter: *Hypothema*, 79
Scheck, Gustav, 6
Schott: music publishers, 19; recorders, 19
Scott, Cyril, 13
serialism, 37, 48, 51–2, 70–1, 79
Serocki, Kazimierz, 18, 104, 118; *Arrange-
ments*, 59, 90, 104, 108, 109, 114, 118;
Concerto alla Cadenza, 115
shakuhachi, 16, 19, 67, 69, 100, 122
Shaw, George Bernard, 2, 6
Shinohara, Makoto: *Fragmente*, 14, 57–9,
58, 89, 99, 118

178

General index